First published 2003 by Contender Books
Contender Books is a division of
The Contender Entertainment Group
48 Margaret Street
London W1W 8SE
www.contendergroup.com/books

This edition published 2003
1 3 5 7 9 10 8 6 4 2

© Contender Entertainment Group 2003

All rights reserved.
No part of this publication may be reproduced, stored in a retrieval system,
or transmitted in any form, or by any means, electrical, mechanical,
photocopying, recording or otherwise without the prior permission of the
publisher or a licence permitting restricted copying.

ISBN 1 84357 095 5

Cover pictures © PA Photos (front), Ken Goff (back).
Inside pictures © Ken Goff, Rex Features, Splash.

Printed in the UK by Bath Press, Bath
Design: Jimmy Egerton
Writing/research: Teresa Maughan
For Contender Books: Kate Gribble

CONTENTS

Chapter One	Justin Timberlake Superstar!	**4**
Chapter Two	Early Years	**14**
Chapter Three	*NSYNC	**22**
Chapter Four	Pop Life	**32**
Chapter Five	The Making Of *Justified*	**44**
Chapter Six	Justin Loves Britney	**56**
Chapter Seven	Justin In Britain	**68**
Chapter Eight	Chillin' Out	**78**
Chapter Nine	The Future	**90**

Chapter One
JUSTIN TIMBERLAKE SUPERSTAR!

"To say that [Michael Jackson] doesn't **inspire me** would be like walking out on stage with a **Band-Aid** on my face and saying I wasn't trying to **look like Nelly**."

"I really **miss my family**. Being with my mother, my dad, my brothers. I **hardly ever** get to see them any more."

He's tall, dark and handsome and exudes charisma, sex and style from every pore. He's got a voice to die for and has more moves than a chess champion. He was brought up in Memphis, Tennessee, and from the moment he drew his first breath this boy was destined for superstardom. With Southern charm and Memphis magnetism, Justin Timberlake is the brightest singing sensation to hit the world in decades.

Talent like this doesn't come along often, but amazingly Memphis can boast not one, but two musical superstars that fit the above description. The first, of course, is 'The King': Elvis Presley, born in nearby Tupelo on 8th January 1935, who was discovered and made his home in the city. On a cold winter's evening on the last day of January, 46 long years later, a second musical genius arrived: Justin Randall Timberlake, the 'Prince of Pop'.

At 22, Justin has already asserted himself as the world's most successful male artist of the new millennium, throwing off the shackles of simply being Britney Spears' boyfriend and one fifth of American boyband *NSYNC, to make his own distinctive mark in music. And who knows what's to come?

Like Elvis, music played an important part in Justin's life while growing up, and he has that same instinct for making black music accessible to all. He's been described by musicians like Jimmy Jam and Brian McKnight as "a black man trapped in a white body," and the latter, who co-wrote the track 'Never Again' on the multi-platinum *Justified*, has no doubts about Justin's superstar potential. "He's one of the most talented young musical artists we have," he enthuses, adding: "He could be the next Elvis."

The similarities to The King don't end there, either, as Justin's biggest musical influence also came from the church. "I got into gospel music and saw a lot of gospel concerts," he reveals. His producer, multi-talented Pharrell Williams of the Neptunes, thinks it shows: "Justin could have been raised in the black church," he says. "He's a great singer, a great talent." Justin also admits to being heavily influenced by R&B. "There's the big blues appeal that goes through Memphis. I mean, it's the city of blues. It's BB King. It's everything. Elvis, he sang blues. I think it's just the whole vibe that went through there. That's where I got the bluesy sound to the way I sing." And it's that voice that put him on the road to fame.

He may only be 22 but Justin Timberlake has already hit the big time on both sides of the Atlantic. Having spent seven years in the limelight as a part of multi-platinum boyband *NSYNC with chart-topping hits like 'Tearin' Up My Heart' and 'Girlfriend', and super-selling albums like *No Strings Attached* and *Celebrity* behind him, Justin has branched out on his own and produced one of the biggest-selling debut albums of recent times.

The album, aptly entitled *Justified*, was released in November 2002 by the Jive record label and reached number two in the US *Billboard* charts behind Eminem's *8 Mile*, selling 439,000 copies in the first week. It went multi-platinum shortly afterwards and is destined to become an all-time classic. In the UK, *Justified* entered the charts at number six and steadily climbed to the top spot, spurred on by the success of second single 'Cry Me A River'. The song, which rocked the pop world because of its controversial video as much as its musical content, reached number two to match the performance of debut single 'Like I Love You'.

But it's not just the sales figures that confirm Justin's position as Planet Pop's hottest new star. In *Justified*, he has produced a ground-breaking album that proves he has enormous songwriting talent – and the accolades have poured in from critics and fans alike. Dubbed "the new Michael Jackson" by many, Justin admits Michael has had a huge influence on him both as a performer and singer. "To say that he doesn't inspire me would be like walking out on stage with a Band-Aid on my face and saying I wasn't trying to look like Nelly," he says.

Remarkably, *Justified* has been described as the album Jacko should have made at the height of his success in the 1980s. Modesty prevents Justin believing the comparisons are wholly warranted, but he smilingly confesses, "I'd have to say I am flattered. It's nice to be compared to someone who is a living legend." Justin's interest in dancing was also inspired by a Jackson, namely Michael's sister Janet, when he saw her 1990 Rhythm Nation Tour. "I went and saw her at the Mid-South Coliseum and was intrigued with how she worked the stage," recalls Justin.

Many also see similarities with Robbie Williams – most obviously because he was another boyband refugee to progress to solo superstar status. And indeed, both Robbie and Justin exhibit that natural charisma and boyish charm that make them irresistible to everyone they meet. Yet unlike Williams, who struggled manfully in the pop wilderness for two years before rising majestically from the Take That ashes, Timberlake has found instant success and adoration.

His transformation from pretty boy to sex god has been

a smooth one, his urban hip-hop style of music giving him true street cred. And, having co-written all 13 tracks on the album, his songwriting talents are beyond doubt. "Musically I've been influenced by artists like Michael Jackson, Prince, Stevie Wonder," he says. "I also listen to singers like Donny Hathaway, Marvin Gaye and Al Green…"

Critics have been universal in their praise for his first solo album: "a remarkable achievement for one so young", "inventive and instant, grindingly raw and sexy, it's a truly great record", "a kick-ass chunk of funky pop" and "this cements Justin's place as one of pop's hottest properties" are just some of the many plaudits. Justin has proved that he is his own person and has a unique style all his own, despite the media's initial insistence that he was just another boyband member trying to manufacture a solo career.

> "Musically I've been influenced by artists like **Michael Jackson, Prince, Stevie Wonder**… I also listen to singers like **Donny Hathaway, Marvin Gaye** and **Al Green**…"

Neptunes producer Chad Hugo has real respect for him. "I think people want to put him in a box, a boyband box, or an *NSYNC box, but he's not like that. He's a real individual and a dope vocalist."

It isn't just the music that has launched Justin into the pop stratosphere however – it's the whole package that gives him his unique appeal, as Quddus, host of MTV's Total Request Live, appreciates. "He's got a flock of girls hollering about how hot he is, he's smart, he can dance – and he really, genuinely, has a voice. He has all the elements of a dynamic artist."

Even in *NSYNC Timberlake had that extra star quality that marked him as the one to watch, despite being the band's youngest member. He first showed the world a glimpse of his songwriting abilities when he penned the monster smash hits 'Gone', 'Girlfriend' and 'Pop' on the group's latest album Celebrity. Even at the tender age of 16, with that mop of blond curly hair and oh-so-innocent blue eyes, Justin was singled out by the fans to be the centre of their attention.

He was regularly mobbed, though he couldn't see what all the fuss was about. "Honestly, I don't look at myself as sexy. I'm just having fun doing what I love and if someone looks at me in that way it's very flattering," he said at the time. He was voted Favourite Male Sex Symbol and Favourite Male Performer in Teen Beat magazine's 17th Annual Teen Star Awards. Friend and fellow band-member JC knows why: "He's got that star quality. When people see Justin on stage, they think he's cool."

Neither did Justin think *NSYNC would become such a global pop phenomenon. "Never in my wildest dreams did I imagine something this big happening," he once said, not foreseeing for a moment that the process would be repeated and that he would, one day, become a legend in his own right.

Having grown from boy to man with the world's press watching, Justin has shown himself to be mature beyond his years. 2002 in particular was a gruelling and emotional time for him, with the coincidence of his very public and bitter break-up with pop princess Britney Spears and his first solo venture away from his *NSYNC pals. Not only has he come through it a wiser and more rounded person, he's also managed to up his street cred a hundredfold.

And Timberlake's appeal is currently stronger than ever. Those awards just keep rolling in. He's been voted one of the top 50 most eligible bachelors in People magazine, and he is currently the pop world's most-wanted cover star, having appeared on the front of top US magazines like Rolling Stone, Vibe, Details, Teen People, Seventeen and Entertainment. He also has the accolade of being only the second male star to grace the cover of Britain's own Marie Claire – the first was David Beckham.

Justin Timberlake may have it all – a sexy body, great looks, pure talent and a fun-loving personality – but he hasn't reached the dizzy heights he's at now through these qualities alone. Two vital ingredients have made him the superstar he is. The first is commitment. He admits he has worked his butt off and still keeps up the pressure on himself, as colleagues like Chad Hugo are quick to point out. "He's a really hard worker. He would stay up late every night just to finish up backing vocals."

The singer agrees he's put in the hours. "My mom always said to me, 'If you're gonna do it, don't do it half-assed.' You've got to give 150 per cent and work for it to get 100 per cent back." Secondly, Justin has that all-important X factor. That indefinable something extra – charisma, charm, magic – whatever it is, Justin has it by the lorryload. "You either have it or you don't," says his old singing coach, Bob Westbrook. "When he was eight years old he did his first performance for his school and the girls were screaming for him then just like they do now. He loved the stage, even then."

The road to stardom hasn't been an easy one, though. Justin has made many sacrifices to achieve his A-list celebrity status. Being in a pop group means being away from home touring or performing and that's hard. "I really miss my family. Being with my mother, my dad, my brothers. I hardly ever get to see them any more. Sometimes it makes me sad because every time I go home my brothers are a foot taller than the last time I saw them. I want to be there for the years that they grow and find out about life."

He also has to make sure he keeps up his fitness levels and the stamina needed for touring – and therefore spends hours shooting basketball and doing push-ups. "I don't smoke cos I'm a singer," he once said, though if you believe the rumours he has been known to let his hair down once in a while.

Rumours aside, there's no doubt whatsoever that Justin Timberlake has worked hard and made many sacrifices to get to where he is in the pop pecking order. And, so far at least, it seems that it's all been worth it.

> **"Honestly, I don't look at myself as sexy. I'm just having fun doing what I love and if someone looks at me in that way it's very flattering."**

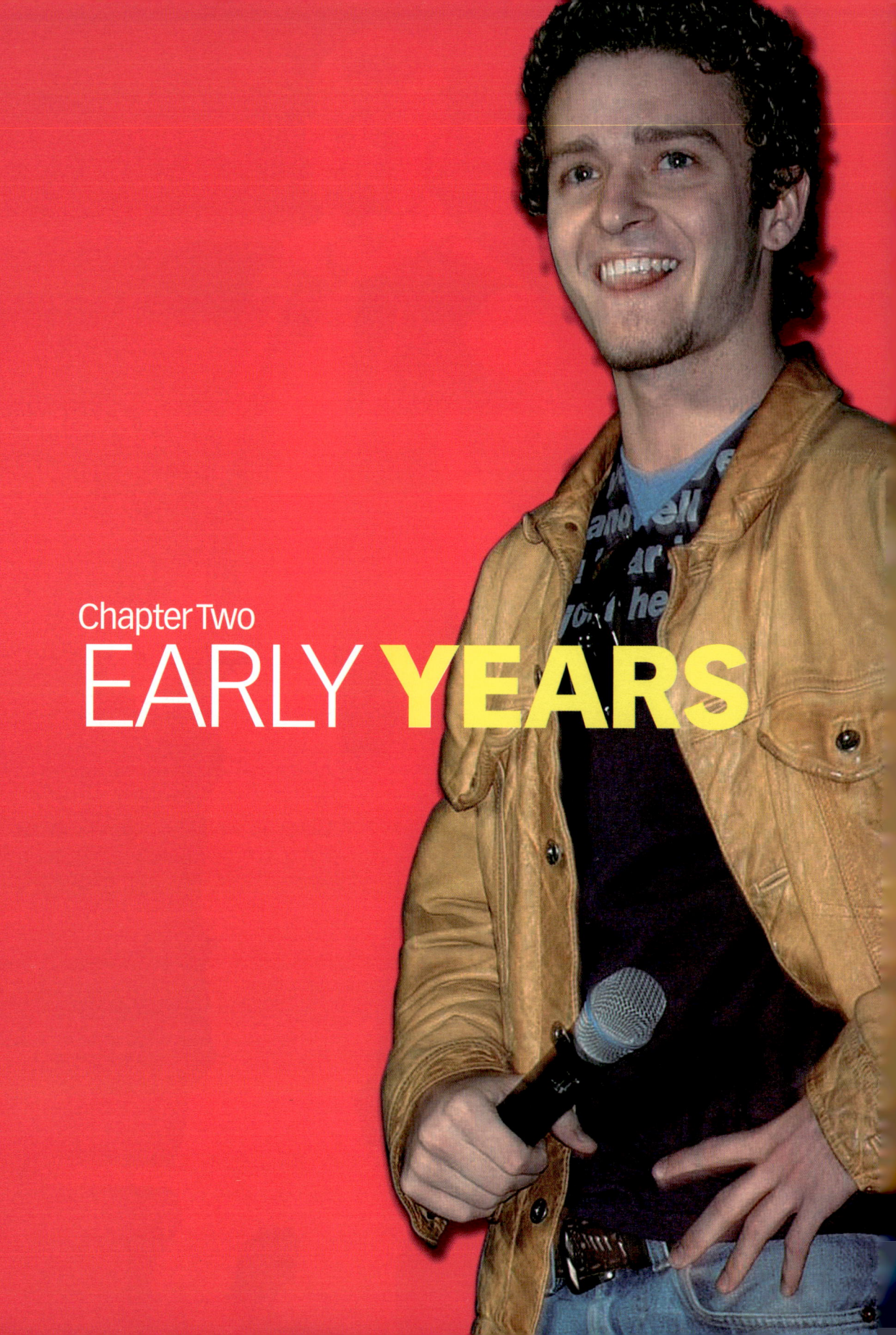

Chapter Two
EARLY YEARS

"After doing some talent shows, **from that moment on**, I knew **performing** was what I wanted to do."

*I*t's 6.30pm on 31 January 1981. A new life has just begun... but who could have predicted that this little bundle of joy would become one of the world's most successful pop stars, barely 19 years on?

Justin Randall Timberlake was born deep in the heart of blues country in Memphis, Tennessee, the first child to mother Lynn and father Randy.

His musical talent was apparent from an early age – at only two years old, his mum caught him singing along in harmony with the car radio. His parents would watch in amazement as, when they played alternately fast and slow records, he would tap his little feet perfectly in time to the music.

Justin probably inherited his amazing voice from dad Randy, who was a singer in a bluegrass band. "Justin was surrounded by music from the day he was born," he recalled. "We never had to teach him to sing; even as a toddler, he would sing and dance for us. When he was just two or three he would jump on the stage when my band were playing and pretend to play his favourite toy guitar." Justin clearly remembers this early love for performing. "If I could talk, I could sing. I was always performing for somebody." His uncle agrees: "Whether he was telling a joke, or dancing in front of everybody at Christmas, Justin was always the entertainer."

Unfortunately, Justin's parents divorced when he was

"Me and my mom have an **understanding**... We're best friends. She knows me better than anyone; **not** a day goes by when I don't talk to her."

very young and both later remarried. His mum wed his stepfather Paul Harless, to whom Justin is very close, while Randy married stepmother Lisa; the couple have two boys. His stepbrothers, Jonathan and Steven, call him 'Big Baba' and Justin "loves them to bits". He also had a sister called Laura Katherine who, sadly, died at only three minutes old. Justin calls her his "Angel in Heaven".

His parents' separation so early in his young life had an understandably traumatic effect on Justin, and he and his mother grew incredibly close. She is now his manager and travels the world with her superstar son. "Me and my mom have an understanding," he explains. "We're best friends. She knows me better than anyone, and not a day goes by

when I don't talk to her." He even has a tattoo on his back of an angel holding a banner with her initials on it. His grandmother, Sadie Bomar, explains how close they are. "The divorce was hard on Justin. It's very confusing for a boy… He couldn't understand why [his daddy] wasn't there any more."

Justin didn't see much of Randy while he was growing up, something his dad understandably now feels bad about: "I lost a lot of quality time with Justin which I will always regret." Now they are on good terms, but Justin's hectic schedule makes meeting up difficult. "We get on well, but I admit I haven't stayed as close as I would have liked to." Justin's grandma believes that "You can never make up for so much lost time from such a crucial period in a life", but adds that the family are close and know that no matter how big a star Justin becomes they all mean the world to him. And they obviously do. "You have to keep your family close… my mom and my grandparents and my dad, all of my family, they all are so, so proud of me. But I'm still Justin to them. I'm still just that little kid who used to run around and act like a little smart alec."

It's this close-knit family which seems to keep him grounded. "I'm close to my mother. I'm close to my father and that's definitely had an impact on my life, seeing how crazy it's got and how my work schedule kind of dictates my life. So I think that it's definitely been a bonus for me to grow up in such a great home and to still be so close to my family. Rest assured, I'm the same dude."

In those early years, Justin went to school like any other kid and had all the same insecurities. "I was always questioning myself in anything and everything. A lot of times people think before they act, and I think sometimes they should act before they think. We should just use our hearts and go for it!" His favourite subject was science and he loathed maths. But his first love was music and, uninspired by the school's own curriculum, Justin begged his mother to let him have singing lessons outside school. "There was a music programme, but it was stupid. If it wasn't for me urging my mom to let me have voice lessons and let me do talent shows, I would never have been here."

It was this lack of inspired music teaching in schools that prompted the young star to set up the Justin Timberlake Foundation – a non-profit making group that gives public schools money for music and arts education. He explains, "My inspiration for doing this was, back when I was ten or eleven in a public school, I had dreams of being in a pop group or being a superstar entertainer, and there was never any music programme to help me pursue my dreams. So I think this giving back is just to make sure that the kids who have those same dreams get the opportunities I didn't have at such a young age. You know, kids really are our future."

Justin's mother hired vocal coach Bob Westbrook to teach her talented young son how to sing, an arrangement that lasted for three years until he was about 11. Justin is very grateful to him for his help. "I grew up singing in church, then I got voice lessons when I was about eight. There is a definite, different way you breathe when you sing. And things that have to happen with your body that you're not

used to. He definitely taught me those things."

After his parents' divorce, Justin and his mum moved to Florida and it was there that his career was given a kick-start. He began entering talent contests and nabbed the top prize for the first time in 'Dance Like The New Kids On The Block' when he was only eight. At ten years old he made a guest appearance on the *Grand Ole Opry*, a country music show in which Justin sang a Southern song to show his heritage. "After doing some talent shows, from that moment on, I knew performing was what I wanted to do," he recalls.

The world caught its first glimpse of Justin the entertainer on his first ever TV appearance on a programme called *Star Search* in Nashville at the age of 11. As fate would have it, Justin failed to go all the way, despite being awarded three and a quarter stars. Nevertheless, he redoubled his efforts, certain he'd succeed one day soon.

The big break that would change his life finally came in 1992, when Justin auditioned for a part on the *New Mickey Mouse Club (MMC)*, a variety show on the Disney Channel that launched in 1989. "I was called in with 200 other kids who had been chosen from 20,000 across America. It was a big deal." He beat the other young hopefuls to become one of 20 regular presenters, and it was here that he first met *NSYNC band member JC (Joshua Scott Chasez) and shared his first on-screen kiss with Britney Spears.

It was also here that he first met Christina Aguilera, though back then he had no inkling that just ten years later he would embark on a massive tour with her, much to the irritation of his now ex-girlfriend Britney. Justin is keen to downplay any controversy, though. "Christina's got one of the most amazing voices I've ever heard," he said in 2003. "That homegirl can sing. She can release a song like 'Dirrty' and get everybody talking, and then release a song like 'Beautiful' and say, 'Look, this is why I am standing here.' That's the Christina I met on the TV show, and that's the Christina that will be around ten years from now."

Justin spent two happy years as one of the 'Mouseketeers' before the show was axed in 1994. He then returned to Memphis with mum Lynn. He is philosophical about *MMC*'s closure. "It was a fluke... If I had won on *Star Search* just one time I would never have made the audition. I just think everything happens for a reason. I think God has His master plan and He'll lay it out for you. But you have to walk that road."

Back in Memphis, Justin returned to EE Jeter Elementary School – but being a "regular kid" was hard to get used to. "I had a good year and a half to be a snotty-nosed kid right after the *Mickey Mouse Club* ended. I was at home from 13, to the summer after when I was 14 and a half. I got so bored and down about everything. I started to get a little rebellious. I didn't really get in trouble, but I wasn't focusing like I could. I didn't have the inspiration that music gave me. That's my place in the world, that's where I belong."

Though he says he got caught experimenting with alcohol and smoking, he seemed to be able to avoid the fallout. "We'd get caught and make sure someone else got in trouble for it." Justin was an achiever academically, too, scoring straight A marks. "I once got a B in seventh grade. I was mad. I was swelled up. I couldn't believe it." Both teachers and students liked him.

Young Master Timberlake's dreams of becoming a superstar still burned bright, however, as did his talent. His grade school teacher Rene Earnest, who went on to work as part of *NSYNC's management team, spotted his amazing ability immediately. "Justin was involved in my gifted students programme. When I first met him he'd been away with the *Mickey Mouse Club*, and I'd heard he was a star and kind of pompous, but he was wonderful."

She has no doubts that his success was no accident. "Justin observes the mechanics of everything in life. He gets the reputation of being snobby or elitist, but it isn't that – he's just very shy. And he's extremely competitive. If he can't win, or figure out how to win, he's not going to play. It's not a negative thing at all; it's just that he likes to conquer things in life." It seems he's always been an achiever; he was president of his middle school's Beta Club and president of the student club at junior high school.

It wasn't all work, though, as Justin was one of those characters always game for a laugh. "I wasn't the type of class clown who was always in trouble," he insists. "I think I was a Ferris Bueller type of clown. I somehow found a way not to get in trouble." He had his darker moments and, like any teenager, came in for his fair share of schoolboy taunts. "I hated my hair," he recalls. "That was the thing everybody teased me about. They called me 'Brillo Pad'. I was always trying to straighten it or cut it all off. I couldn't deal with it. In second grade, I took paper scissors and just cut my hair all uneven. I was like, 'I can't stand this! Snip, snip, snip.' That's the only time I ever really got a spanking."

Throughout this time, Justin kept in touch with his old Mouseketeer mates, and it was in a roundabout way that *NSYNC was formed. "JC and I got chatting when we were on the *MMC* show and discovered that we both wanted to be in a band. I mentioned it to Chris [Christopher Alan Kirkpatrick] who was an old buddy from auditioning," Justin now recalls. Chris was working at Universal Studios with a guy called Joey (Joseph Anthony Fatone Jr) who also happened to be an old mate of Justin's – and it didn't take long for him to become involved.

Together the foursome had a great vocal range... but if their vision of putting together a band that could sing *a cappella* and transform five-part harmonies into pure pop were to become a reality, they would need a good bass. Step forward Justin's old vocal coach Bob Westbrook, who gave the boys the number of a young lad who loved to sing. The quartet knew they had found their "missing voice"

"I **hated my hair**. That was the thing everybody teased me about. They called me **'Brillo Pad'**. I was always trying to straighten it or **cut it all off**."

as soon as they heard his first few notes, and the quintet was formed. "I was really into singing and some friends encouraged me to sing with the local choir, which is how the others heard about me," revealed the lucky Lance (real name James Bass).

So they had a group, but what about a name? The boys really struggled, playing around with different ideas but never coming up with something that suited them. It was actually Justin's mum who came up with the name *NSYNC after idly remarking that when it came to their harmonies and dance moves the boys really were "in sync". The phrase struck a chord with the guys, but they weren't convinced until Justin's mum had played around with their names and formed *NSYNC from the last letter of each of their names – JustiN, ChriS, JoeY, LansteN and JC. She had to cheat a bit with Lance, as he explains: "That's how I got my nickname. The last letter of my real name didn't fit in *NSYNC so Justin made a big joke about calling me Lansten... and it kinda stuck."

Justin was only 14 when *NSYNC formed and still at high school, so he had to study by day and practise his dance moves by night. Joey would get off work at nine in the evening and they'd rehearse in a disused warehouse until midnight, performing wherever and whenever they could. But it wasn't long before the work paid off. "We did our demo package as fast as we could," Justin recalls, "and that's when we got in touch with our management."

Everything from the poster printing, the outfits, the order of songs and the choreography was done by the five alone. "It was very rough, but we did it ourselves," agrees Chris. The demo had a few original tracks and a funky cover version of the Beatles song 'We Can Work It Out'. The boys had no doubt that they would soon be flying high. "From day one, I knew it was going to work,' said Lance. "The first time we sang together I was like, 'This is it!'"

*NSYNC's phenomenal success meant that Justin could barely fit schoolwork into his hectic schedule, and he was put on a fast-track study programme specifically designed for performers and competitive athletes. At the time Justin said, "It's hard to make myself study when the other guys are hangin' out and having fun, but I want to finish school as soon as possible so I can focus my full attention on my entertainment career." And finish school he did. Justin graduated from high school via mail, a year early, in 1998. He'd always intended to go back to further education when he got the chance but, with the prospect of international success, wads of cash, and doing a job he loves, there seems little chance of that now.

And why should he? Only five years after graduating, Justin is one of the world's wealthiest and most respected music stars – and there's no college in the world that can teach you that!

Chapter Three
*NSYNC

"Being on stage every night is **great**, every night is different. We're getting to see the world in a great way and we're **very blessed** that everything has gone as well as it has."

It was 1996 when *NSYNC's world collided with that of Johnny Wright, the mastermind behind groups like the Backstreet Boys and New Kids On The Block. And, after that timely collision, they set off on a new path to fame and fortune from which they have never once looked back. After receiving a call from partner Lou "Big Papa" Pearlman recommending he check out a new band, Johnny flew to Orlando to see what all the fuss was about. "I discovered a band who really could sing and had a chemistry or aura about them," he recalls.

Wright landed them a record deal with German-based company BMG – so it was off to Europe to start recording their first album. Justin had just turned 15 and, though he was still the baby of the band, he worked just as hard as the other guys at perfecting the choreography and belting out those tunes. Their debut album *NSYNC was released in Europe in 1997 and the debut single 'I Want You Back' stormed up the charts straight into the Top Ten. Within a few weeks it would not only go gold but also capture the title of 'longest reign in the charts for a new act'. Next single up, 'Tearin' Up My Heart', also raced into the Top Five and earned the boys another gold disc. It wasn't long before the self-named *NSYNC album went gold and the band had made its mark. Now all they had to do was conquer Britain and their homeland.

Despite their success in mainland Europe, a breakthrough in the UK eluded the band; the first single flopped badly, which wasn't much of a surprise since its release date was the day after Princess Diana died. But their grit and determination wasn't about to run out just yet. "It was important for us to break in the UK. So we gave it some time, came back a year and a half later and succeeded," Justin says. And success tasted all the sweeter when the single 'I Want You Back' hit the Top Five.

Attention turned to the biggest market of all – the boys' native country, America. Stateside success may have taken a little time but, when it came, it was massive! The first two singles sold well, but the band didn't make a big impact on the music scene until their appearance in a Disney Channel concert in July 1998. Ironically, rivals the Backstreet Boys gave them their lucky break when they turned down the opportunity to appear. From that moment on, *NSYNC never looked back. They were an instant hit – the fan mail poured in and they had to get a trolley to shift it! The debut album notched up ten million sales earning the boys a well-deserved platinum disc. *NSYNC were hot property…

Five friends, united in their love for music and performing, had finally seized the hearts and minds of music fans across the globe, with their unique blend of harmonising vocals and energetic dance moves. The roller coaster ride went into overdrive and the offers poured in. *NSYNC the album had produced a staggering four Stateside number one singles with 'I Want You Back', 'Tearin' Up My Heart', 'God Must Have Spent A Little More Time On You' and 'I Drive Myself Crazy'.

It was time to go on tour… and what better place to kick off than where it had all begun – back in Orlando, Florida? Since Justin's old pal and fellow Mouseketeer Britney Spears was the opening act, it really was like coming home. 1999 brought even more fame for the quintet with the launch of a new tour (all of whose 100 dates quickly sold out), numerous TV appearances and an avalanche of awards.

But it wasn't all to be good news, as the boys' decision to leave record label RCA/BMG and manager Lou Pearlman was to lead to a long and bitter legal battle. An enraged Lou filed a $150,000 million lawsuit for breach of contract against the feisty five, and they hit back with a counter-suit of their own. The wrangle was eventually settled out of court but, as Justin reveals, it was a hard thing to go through. "It was horrible. That was my biggest low point."

Timberlake is candid about why they felt it was time to move on, explaining that there had been a misunderstanding about the compensation Lou should receive for setting the band on the route to success. "When we got this group together, we came to Lou and he said he would back us financially. It was a big rush. But we were the ones who sat around till three in the morning singing together and hanging out together and doing the things friends do. The money Lou dished out he got back within the first six months of our success, and the first record. A few records had gone by since then, and we were still in the same situation."

He has no regrets, and admits that the experience is probably responsible for his fixation on retaining control of his career. At 19 he had learnt a hard lesson and, as a solo performer, he now demands and receives complete creative control from his record company.

Legal matters safely sorted, it was time to hit the studio to record album number two, *No Strings Attached*. Released in March 2000 it was a monster hit, smashing all records with sales of 2.4 million in a week and spawning yet another number one with 'Bye, Bye, Bye'. It was the first time an

album had sold more than two million copies in a single week and easily beat the Backstreet Boys' previous record of 1.13 million. The album went straight to the top of the *Billboard* 200 where it was to remain for the next eight weeks. It has since sold over 11 million copies to be certified not merely platinum but diamond.

"It was a challenge doing this record," Justin admitted at the time. "Picking out the right songs that fit where you want to go musically; where you want to take your fans. We went through a lot of things in 1999 and we went through them really fast. We have a very broad sound and there are some different directions we can take it, so we did as much of that as we could on this album. That's why we called the album *No Strings Attached*. We have no strings to hold us down. We're ready to show the world that."

Launched in May in Biloxi, the sell-out No Strings Attached Tour kicked off in spectacular fashion. Over one million tickets were sold in the first day, with 51 out of 52 gigs selling out immediately. The 90-minute live show was a knockout – a poptastic extravaganza of energetic choreography, stunning special effects and mind-blowing music. Forty-one cities and three months later, the boys arrived in New York tired but elated, to play four sensational gigs at the legendary Madison Square Garden venue.

Touring had brought international recognition and put the boys in their element. As Justin enthused at the time, "Being on stage every night is great, every night is different. We're getting to see the world in a great way and we're very blessed that everything has gone as well as it has. We enjoy riding on nice buses and meeting nice people." As 2000 came to a close, *NSYNC had earned their place as one of the music industry's biggest earners, reportedly raking in a whopping $184 million during the year, beating the likes of Eminem, Britney Spears and the Backstreet Boys – as well as more established artists like Tina Turner and Sting.

If 2000 was the year that cemented *NSYNC as the biggest teen band in history, then 2001 was the year that witnessed their metamorphosis into a group of musicians with club-scene clout who could bring their teen fans with them. After winning the MTV Music Award for Best Pop Video 2000 and Viewers' Choice with 'Bye, Bye, Bye', the boys would follow up with even more awards in the coming year.

*NSYNC's third album, *Celebrity*, came out in July 2001 and sold 3.3 million copies in the first three weeks of release. It was this album that changed people's perception of the band and introduced Justin as an accomplished songwriter and producer. He co-wrote seven and co-produced five of the tracks, many with band choreographer Wade J. Robson. "We got together and wrote for a week," Justin revealed, "and came up with 'Pop', 'Celebrity', 'See Right Through You', and 'Gone'. It's crazy. We've got a chemistry that's second to none."

It was the chaos of those first few years in *NSYNC that inspired the title *Celebrity*. "It's not how we look at ourselves, but we know that's how a lot of people see us, because they don't get to meet us. That's why the album sleeve is all glitzy on the outside, whereas inside it's us in

"The coolest thing about songwriting is to know it started with this little guitar riff, and the next thing you know it's being played on the radio."

very natural settings, in black and white, shot in documentary style. It's me drinking a cup of coffee just waking up. That's how we look at our lives. If we weren't in *NSYNC we'd still be who we are."

It was while working on the track 'Girlfriend' that Justin first met pop producers Pharrell Williams and Chad Hugo of the Neptunes. "Pharrell wanted to have a hands-on approach with me in the lyrics. I think I have a special relationship with him. It was easy to write with him because he knows the way I would say something." Producer BT, who also worked on *Celebrity*, was struck by the singer's similarity to another pop legend. "The tonality of Justin's vocals and his rhythmic instincts for really percussive singing are very Michael Jackson," he said at the time.

With so many songs on *Celebrity* carrying the Timberlake stamp, fans saw a new side of the charismatic singer. Critics were surprised at the harder-edged sound of the album, and in particular 'Pop', Justin's take on the pop industry. "I think I was testifying for everyone who does what people consider bubblegum pop — not just us, but Christina, Britney, Backstreet Boys, anybody. First of all, it wasn't meant to be serious, but everyone took those lyrics to heart. But damn it, the music is fun, so get over it. When we do that song, I've never seen people dance so hard in the stadium! They enjoy it. That's the point."

'Pop' was seen by many as too aggressive a sound for the all-boy group from Orlando and many radio stations shied away from playing it, but Justin and the gang weren't perturbed. "We knew that was gonna happen. At the point we're at in our careers, it was like, where do we want to go? For us, this was a growth record. You have to switch it up, every time you go out. That's what makes you an artist — the fact that you make something different each time. Maybe this is our puberty record."

So where does Justin get the inspiration for his music? In songs like 'Pop' it's from the world around him, but in others it just comes from playing about with a tune. He explains, "'Gone', the ballad on *Celebrity*, started off as just a guitar riff and a melody and it became this sad thing, so I wanted to make the concept sad to go with the very dark melody. The coolest thing about songwriting is to know it started with this little guitar riff, and the next thing you know it's being played on the radio."

Ironically, when he wrote 'Gone', Justin was predicting what was to come in his own relationship with Ms Spears. "I wrote that song when Britney and I were a couple and she went to the hair salon and said she'd be back in a couple of hours," he remembers. "When she got there she decided to get a manicure and a pedicure, and wasn't back for five hours or so. That's what gave me the idea for the song. There was this whole idea of, 'I wonder what it would feel like [to have] all that sorrow, to miss someone like that?'" Sadly for Justin, it wouldn't be long before he'd know exactly what it felt like.

With sales of over 30 million records worldwide, *NSYNC had become the undisputed crown princes of pop, as their many awards confirmed. They won four Video Music Awards at the 2001 MTV Video Music Awards — Viewers' Choice, Best Pop Video, Best Group Video and Best Dance Video. Even better, Justin's idol Michael Jackson made a surprise appearance during *NSYNC's MTV performance of 'Pop'. Emerging from a backdrop that stated simply 'King of Pop', he joined the guys in their dance moves, whipping the audience up into an even bigger frenzy. 2003 saw Justin voted Favourite Male Singer at Nickelodeon's 16th Annual Kids' Choice Awards in Santa Monica, California, and he sealed the deal by performing 'Rock Your Body', much to the delight of his fans.

At the time of writing, the guys are having a break from *NSYNC to develop their solo careers, but insist they intend staying together. "We're all doing individual things," says Justin. "Joey's in New York doing a show, and Lance just finished his training [to be an astronaut with NASA]. I keep in contact with them as often as possible. We all have individual lives as well as our commitments to the group." He denies his reason for going solo was to have the final say on everything. "With *NSYNC we have total artistic control anyway, so it isn't that different. It's more a case of me being in total control from my point of view. The decisions are made by one person — me — not five."

So *NSYNC fans shouldn't go tearin' up their hearts just yet. The game isn't over and, with luck, they'll be bringing on da noise, no strings attached, real soon.

Chapter Four
POP LIFE

"I once read an article that **just got me** – and I **totally lost it**. I sat with my mother and I just **cried**. I just broke down."

Globetrotting from New York to Paris to Tokyo to Sydney to London in a private jet. Sipping champagne in the back of a limo surrounded by gorgeous girls. Getting down with artists like Stevie Wonder, Janet Jackson, Brian McKnight and Kylie Minogue. It's all in a day's work for Justin Timberlake, pop's brightest star, so how does he keep those sneaker-clad feet from leaving the ground? And what is it really like to be rich, raunchy and in demand?

It helps to have a family who are there to support you no matter what, and Justin certainly has that. His mother Lynn Harless is his manager and his stepdad helps out with managing the finances, so they're with him every step of the way. Justin acknowledges that family and friends are really important. "My mom is my best friend and there's nothing I have done or that I'm gonna do that my mom doesn't know about," he once said. He talks with his mum every day on the phone if she isn't travelling with him, and she's by his side if he's feeling low. Justin also really enjoys going back home to see his two stepbrothers and just hanging out. "He plays basketball with them for hours, and when he came back last Christmas it was like Santa Claus visiting," recalls dad Randy.

"I do feel homesick when I'm away," confesses Justin. "Sometimes the business can be so hectic and then you're all alone. I work so hard it's crazy. I do loads of stuff in a day and then go back to the hotel room and it's just me by myself. You go to extremes – from really high to really low." He also relies on his faith – he's a Baptist. "When things get kind of weird for me, and they often do, I just turn to my spirituality. It has helped me through a lot of those things."

Justin has been in the spotlight since the age of 12 and has virtually grown up in the glare of paparazzi flashbulbs. Living his life in the public eye isn't always easy, either. "It's real hard having your private life written about and speculated on by total strangers," he says, "but as I've grown up I've learned to not let it bother me and to concentrate on my music. People will write and believe what they like but if they appreciate me musically that's all that counts."

Justin is as famous in the States as David Beckham is in Britain, and his life and loves have become regular tabloid and magazine fodder, while in the UK Justin is fast attracting the attention worthy of a superstar. Luckily, he's come to take what he reads about himself with a pinch of salt. "The [British] tabloids have just grabbed hold of me in the past year. It becomes a little annoying – the fact that people just want to ask personal questions and I'm kind of like, hey, I've got a record coming out too. But I understand that it's just something that comes along with [the business] and I'm cool with it."

He doesn't feel it's his responsibility to live his life in a particular way to please others, or to comment on others' take on him. "I have my own perspective. The only thing that I can do is just laugh about the things that people say about me that aren't true." It hasn't always been this way. When he was younger he sometimes found the gossip hard to deal with. "I once read an article that just got me – and I totally lost it. I sat with my mother and I just cried. I just broke down," he remembers.

But fame has its upsides, too, as Justin is quick to point out. "The best thing is that you can reach so many people with what you do." Being famous allowed him to start the Justin Timberlake Foundation. It is a programme he feels passionate about and has a lot of hands-on involvement in. "I think kids should learn about every different style and era of music, and it should be fun. Classes should include today's music too.

"Every time you give a young person an opportunity to let out their energy in a positive way," he continues, "you're gonna have a better outcome. I mean, say you get a couple of kids who don't fit in, and they go and form a garage band. The next thing you know they're Pearl Jam or Blink 182. It could happen to anyone. It really could." Justin has even the White House, where he was praised by the First Family for his efforts and met Hillary Clinton. "That was cool," he gushes.

His fame has also enabled him to lend his support to other causes that he believes in and he is happy to use his celebrity to make people sit up and take notice. He once appeared in an advertisement promoting gun control – despite his Southern upbringing. He has a very mature take on the situation for one so young. "The constitution used to be my stance on gun control – the right to bear arms and all that. But times are different now. It's one thing to have a musket 200 years ago, to shoot bears and get food to eat, but it's another thing to be 17 today walking around with an AK-47," he says sagely.

Justin also feels strongly about drinking and driving, especially after the death of an *NSYNC fan who, while waiting to catch a glimpse of her idols outside an LA radio station, was knocked down and killed by an allegedly drunk driver. There and then, he decided to front an anti-drink driving campaign. "I really hope it makes a difference. I feel

"My mom is my best friend and there's nothing I have done or that I'm gonna do that my mom doesn't know about."

that if we can change just one person's views or save at least one life then it will have been a success."

Justin has promised never to exploit his fame, even when it might save him from an embarrassing situation. He stuck to his words when he was zapped with a speeding ticket for zipping around town in his new BMW roadster. "I wasn't about to say, 'Hey, do you want an autograph and not give me a ticket?' I was speeding, he caught me, and I learned my lesson," he says fairly.

Fame and fortune do have their advantages though – and, judging by the size of his diamond-studded Minola watch, being able to go into a shop and buy whatever you fancy is one of them. But Justin has a savvy head on those bronzed, muscular shoulders and he's not averse to making the most of his superstar status when it comes to free gear. "The free swag. I love the free swag. The sneakers, the Nikes, the Ponys..." It's not his fault designers are clamouring to send him their latest gear on the off-chance that if he is snapped sporting their logo, sales are likely to increase one thousandfold overnight.

Like trendsetter David Beckham, Justin's perfect features, sexy body and sense of style make him a real fashion icon. Let's face it, Mr Timberlake could wear a tea-towel and look fantastic!

Free clothes aside, Justin's earnings mean that he can buy clothes like they're going out of fashion... and he does! For the record, his favourite stores are Foot Locker, Foot Action, Champs Sports and Abercrombie & Fitch.

When it comes to clothes, Justin goes for a relaxed style that reflects his personality. His sense of style has evolved from schoolboy sportswear to urban chic. His favourite clothing used to be anything from North Carolina in Baby Blue, but nowadays you're more likely to see him in comfy clothes from Abercrombie & Fitch. Even A&F's cologne, Woods, is his favourite. Whether he's hanging out, performing or out on the town he always looks (and smells!) sensational. "I'm a jeans and T-shirt kind of guy," he says. "I just wear what's comfortable. I'll just throw on some vintage jeans and some boots or some sneakers and throw on the T-shirt and be on my way... You have to dress up sometimes, though I wouldn't mind wearing tennis shoes to the Oscars, to be honest."

And there's a reason why! When he was younger his great passion was collecting sneakers – Justin used to take an empty duffel bag with him when he went on the road in case he passed a branch of Foot Locker. "I started collecting Air Jordans," he confesses a little guiltily. "Every year they would come out with a new Air Jordan model and I had to have it." He has over 300 pairs of trainers to date and his collection just keeps growing.

Justin's favourite designers are Robert Cavalli and Dolce & Gabbana, and if you're wondering what he wears underneath those sexy pec-hugging tees and bum-cradling pants then keep wondering. "I don't wear underwear," he claims, though rumours have it he favours Tommy Hilfiger or Calvin Klein boxers. Underneath that, he can claim to have not just a beautiful body but beautiful body art – he has seven tattoos. "I have a cross on my left shoulder. Three tattoos on my right ankle – they represent all the albums *NSYNC released. I have a tribal band with an Aquarius

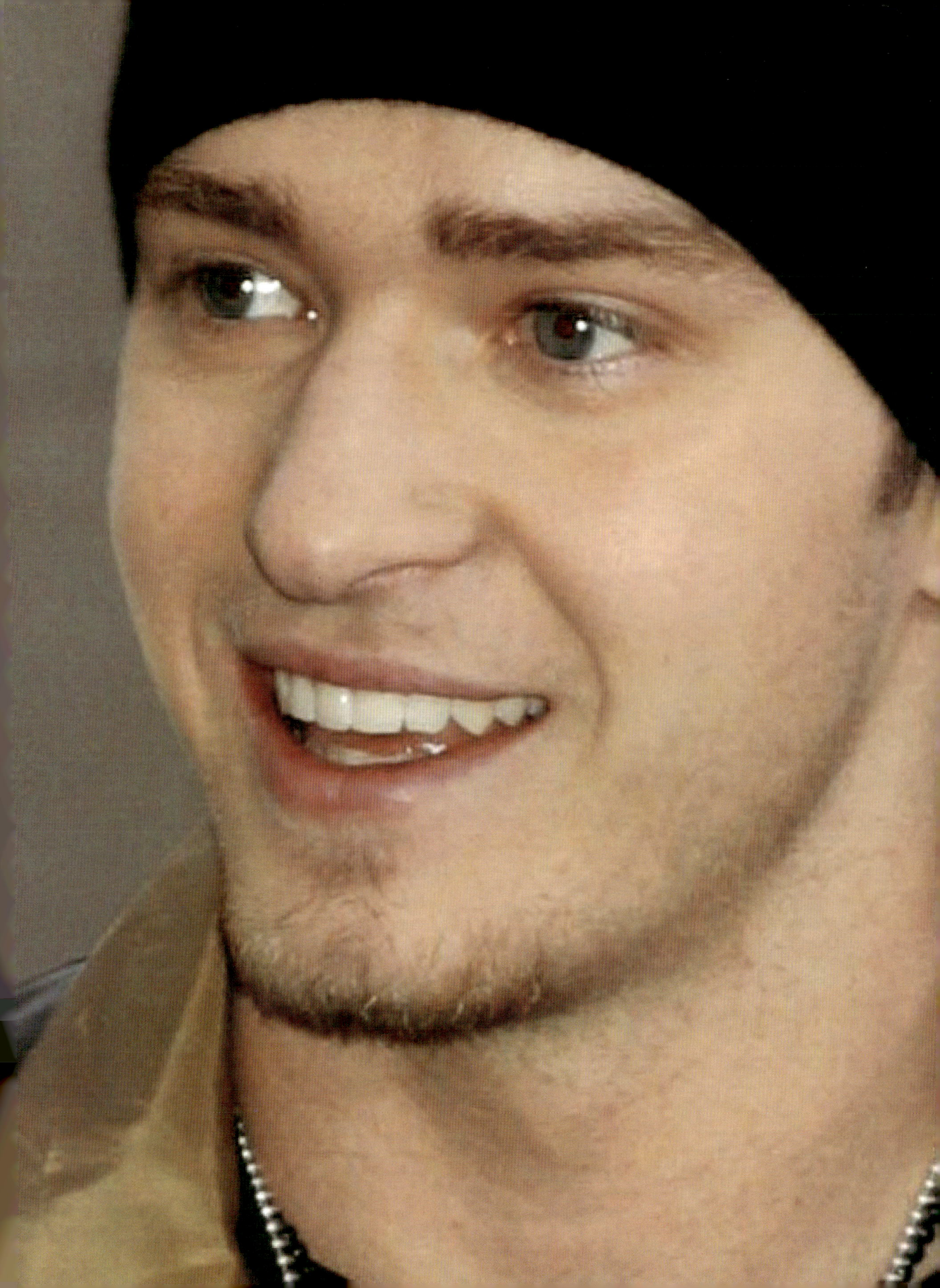

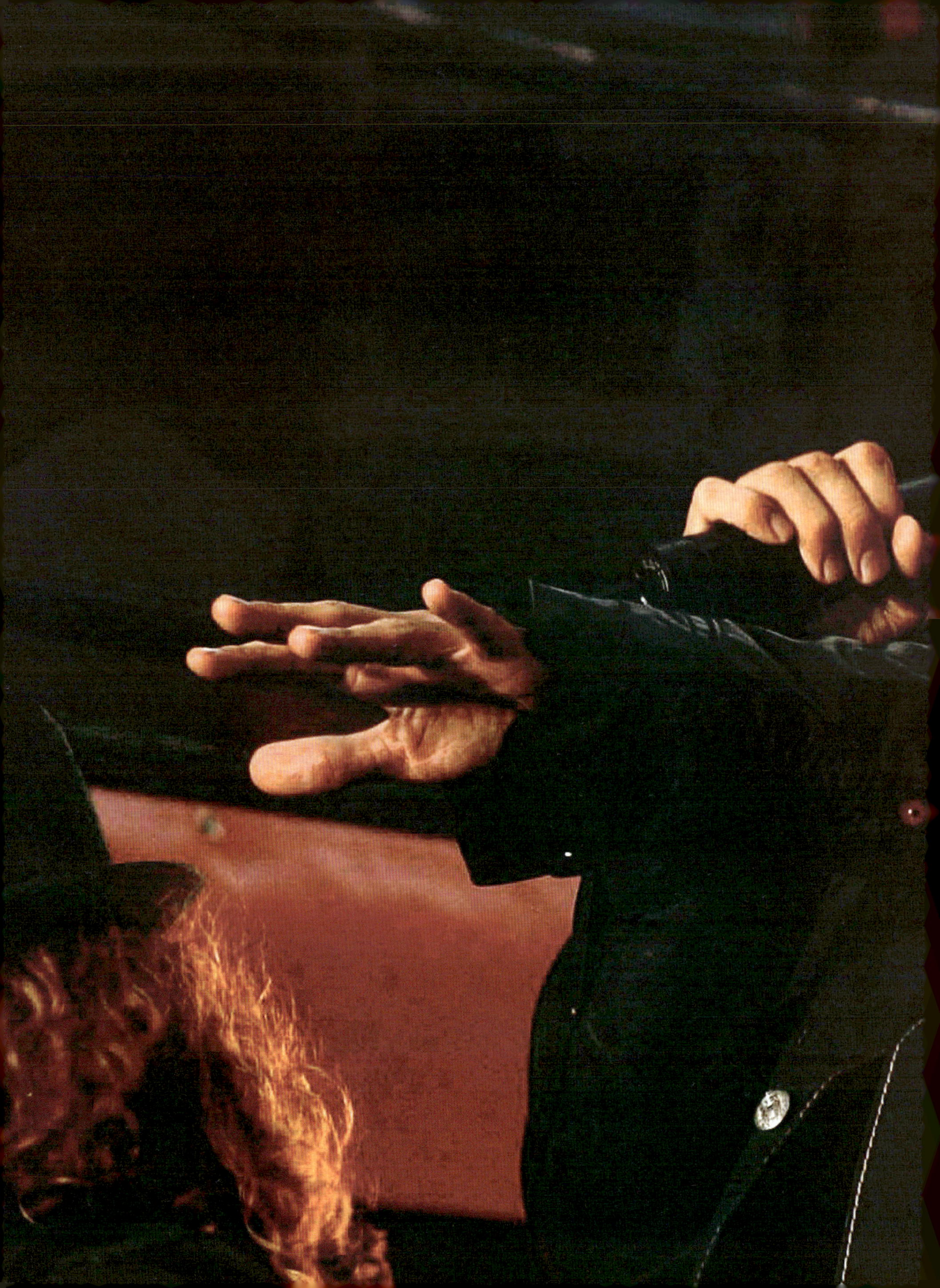

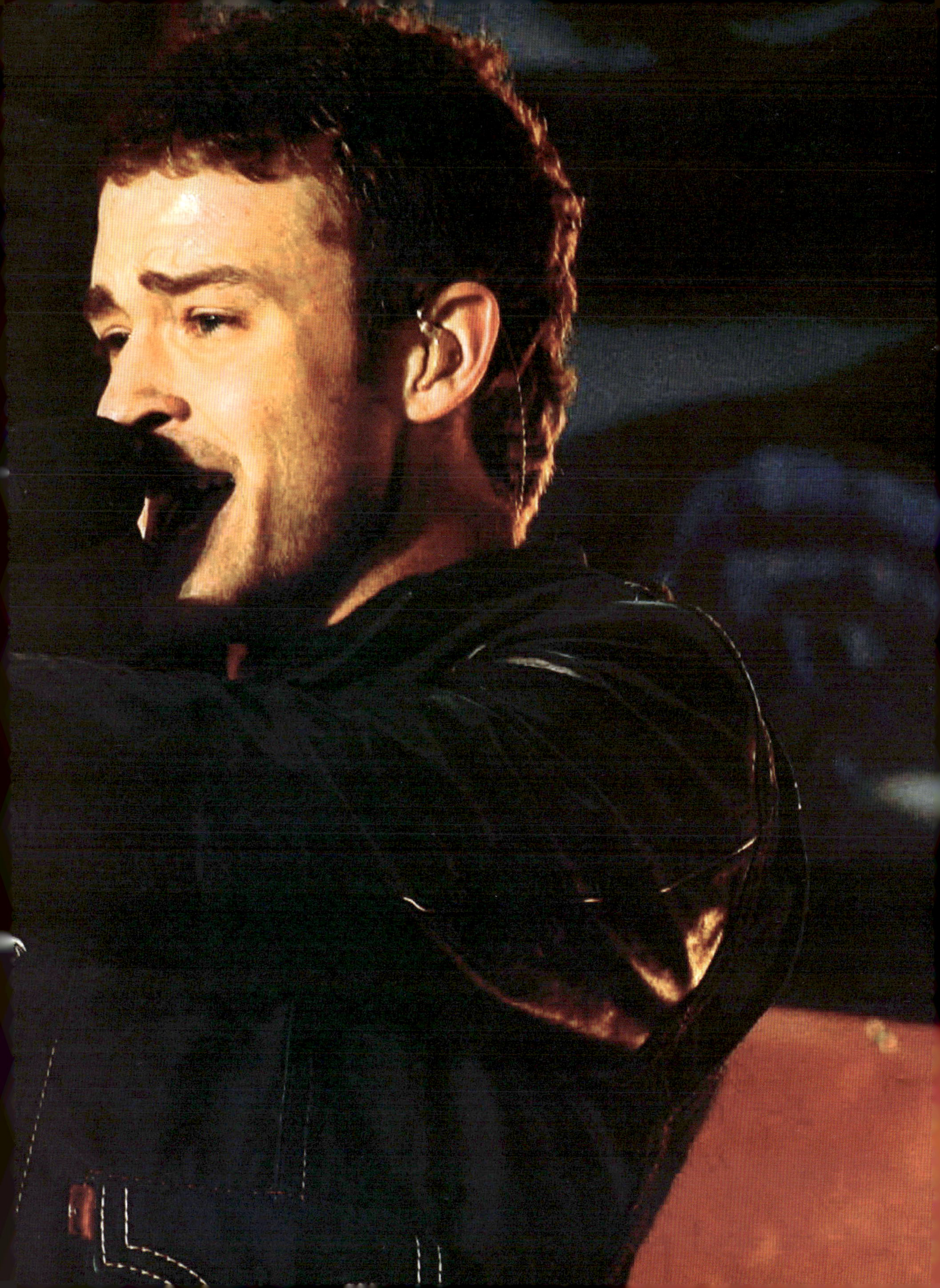

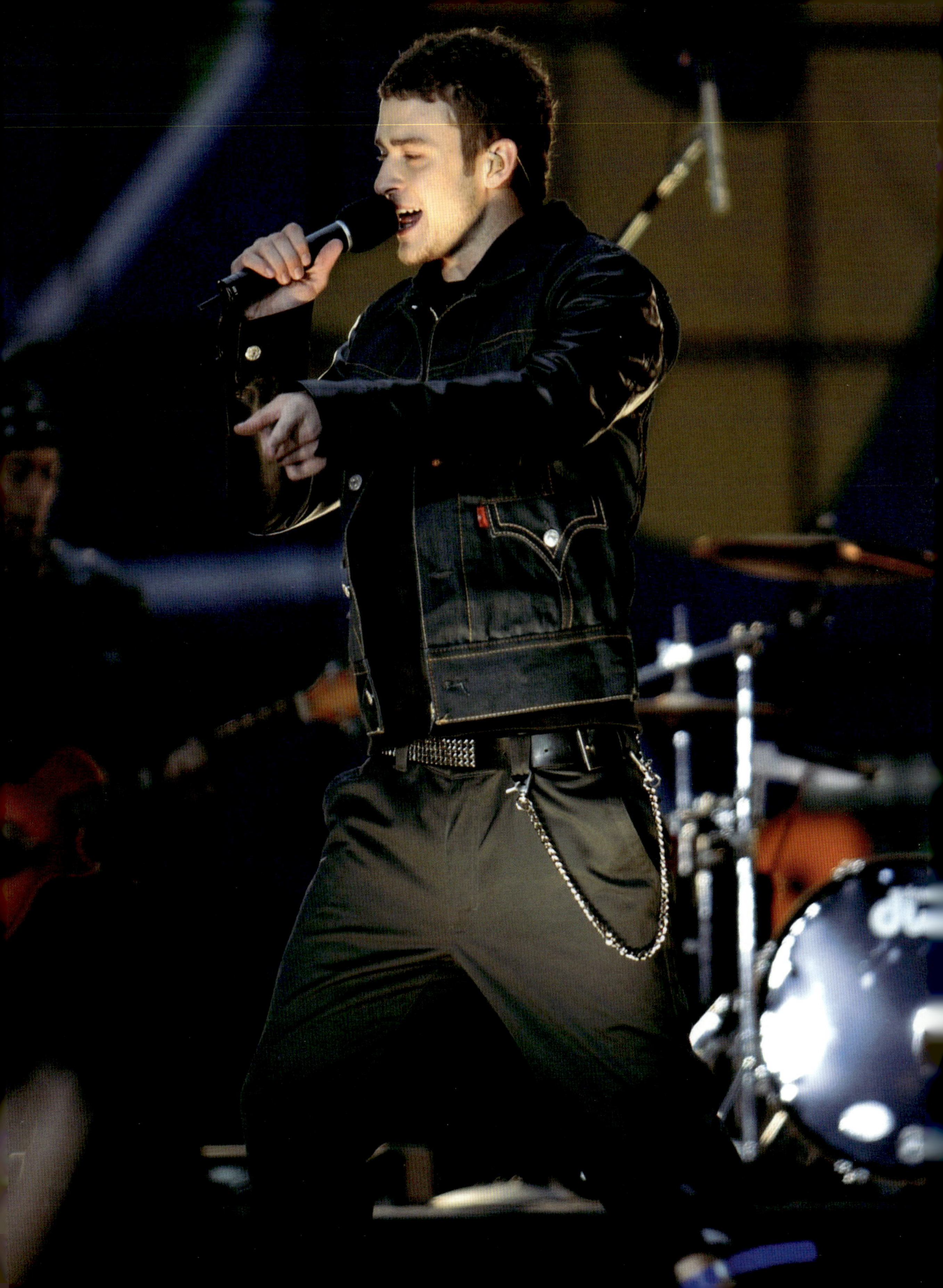

symbol below my knee. And on my left ankle I have a Japanese 'canji' symbol for music or song." He also has an angel on his back.

His tall, lean frame means he can wear almost anything and still look cool, though he does admit to having his own fashion disasters. He once wore a pair of purple Spandex shorts. He recalls, "I looked like I was Patrick Swayze and someone came by me and cut my pants. I've got chicken legs, so it wasn't a sexy look." He reckons his worst recent fashion faux pas was having a bad hair day. "I had the short, bleached Eminem haircut before him. It looks good on him, but it was not working for me. What was I thinking?" he laughs.

Joking aside, if you ask him if there is anything he doesn't like physically about himself, he'll always say his hair. Those bubbly locks that gave him his nickname Curly and were loved by teenage girls everywhere were the bane of his life. He used to get called all sorts at school. He remembers, "I grew my hair out once and I'd wake up every morning and look just like [extravagantly Afro'd soul singer] Maxwell. Whoa! My hair was scaring me!"

Justin also splashes his cash on his other great love – speed – and admits it's a bit of an obsession. "I'm developing this thing for cars," he has confessed. "I've got a maroon Mercedes M-Class truck that's all chromed out. And I've got a blue BMW roadster. It's really, really fast." But nowadays he doesn't have the time to drive them all so he has flogged a few. "I think I had erm… seven… no, eight… or maybe nine." He now drives a Dodge Viper and Cadillac Escalade and also has a top-of-the-range Harley Davidson motorbike.

Cruising down the Pacific Coast Highway, not too fast, not too slow, drinking in the fresh air, he's as free as a bird. Freedom is what it's all about, he says. "That's what the Harley represents, isn't it? Freedom. And in the past year I think it's been the underlying theme in my life – freedom and transition. I've moved into a new house, become a bachelor and started a solo career." He's even bought a Harley each for his mum and stepdad. "We have about seven now. They have two that they keep at their home in Memphis, I have two that I'm keeping at my home in LA, and we have three in the house in Orlando."

Does he enjoy being able to indulge himself and his family like that? Actually, he says, the best thing about the money is that he can treat his parents after they've supported him for two decades. He's also bought a $5 million house in the Hollywood Hills. "It's beautiful. I have ten acres of land and it's been completely landscaped and I have a rose garden, a tennis court and a huge area with willow trees. It looks like an enchanted forest, like something from *Lord Of The Rings*. Me and my mom designed the house ourselves. C'mon, what would your mom do if you said, 'Here's 13,000 square feet, now fill it'? She had a ball!"

Justin is very enthusiastic about his new house, partly because it's given him the chance to stamp his own personality on it (he used to share Britney's mansion) and partly because it's somewhere he can retreat to and chill out away from the pressures of stardom. "The house is kinda shabby chic mixed with Arte de Mexico. It's nice and classy and has a lot of leather, too."

But when it comes to material goods, he does have a sense of perspective. "I think possessions end up possessing you. Though it's fun to have toys – I buy a lot of jewellery." (He created the JRT design for his famed necklace himself.) "I wear necklaces, diamond watches. I like to have fun. I don't have anything that's stuck with me." He reveals that he wouldn't rescue anything if his house was on fire, apart from "maybe a change of clothes".

Justin is just as philosophical about his current celebrity status and is quick to point out that fame is not really that important. "Celebrity is not a word I believe in. I come from a very humble background and believe that people are a product of their upbringing. My mom always taught me that being a good person is the most important thing. So many people play-act at being a celebrity and that's just not the way I want to live my life."

That may be true but, whether he likes it or not, Justin is plagued by paparazzi and followed by his fans wherever he goes. And that means he has the company of an entourage of bodyguards, publicity people and general hangers-on. He finds one of the most difficult things about being a celebrity is not being able to pop out to buy a carton of milk without having an army of minders to protect him from being mobbed.

"That's the only part that bothers me," he admits, "that I do have to take precautions. Sometimes you just wanna go to the movies. I mean, I'm only 22 years old. But it's something you get used to. My perspective of normality is way different to someone else's." He may not believe in celebrity or fame but, as he says, "I do believe in the power of music. I see how people react to it and that's not about me, it's about a piece of pop culture."

He used to rely on his ex to cope with the pressures of celebrity and has said in the past that, when he got depressed, he'd turn to her for comfort. "The best thing I do is soak myself into Britney. She's kind of like my safe haven as far as all of this hoopla goes," he said. Maybe fame is starting to take its toll, as on a recent trip to Britain Justin lost his cool when besieged by fans at hip London restaurant Planet Hollywood. Reports suggested that, despite his eleven bodyguards, fans flocked around Justin as he entered the posh burger bar. Justin allegedly told them "I'm just here for a f***ing burger" and requested screens be put up around his table so he could eat his meal in peace. Not very friendly but we forgive him: Justin is only human, after all.

He confesses that the only irritating thing about being a celebrity is the press, and says the paparazzi are far scarier than his fans. "I can do without the fabrications. They're amusing but, at the same time, they're frustrating. If I didn't say they get on my nerves sometimes that would be dishonest, but it's not do or die. People can say whatever they want, but if your music is hot that speaks for itself. All I can hope for is that people gravitate to what I've done on my latest record. The worst thing about being famous is the invasion of your privacy."

So how does he rise above it all? "How you survive is you don't buy into it. You wake up, you look in the mirror and you say, 'I love you, but you're a funny-ass, ugly dude.' And you make a record for yourself. You say, 'What do I want to hear myself do?' and you hope everybody gravitates towards it. And that's the most rewarding thing about

Justified... because it's been a long time coming and I did it my way."

But it isn't fame and fortune that motivates him. Justin Timberlake loves performing, he always has, and it's that love of being on stage that makes it all worth it. "I love the feeling when you're up there, and the crowd is getting into what you're doing. I love to see smiles on their faces and know that I had something to do with it!"

While in *NSYNC, the boys had two major tours in one year alone – during which Justin made over 300 personal appearances – so he has learned to cope with life away from family and friends. He reveals that, when things got crazy, he could phone his mum. "She was always there to say, 'The moment this feeling goes away, the moment that you stop loving what you do and stop really wanting to do it, then it can just stop.'" But that love of struttin' his stuff, playing the music he adores and meeting new people in new places has never left him. And that's why he's still on the road today.

He says the best present a fan ever gave the band was a star in a constellation named after them. The most complimentary thing someone could say to him is "I love your album, I really respect your music." He hasn't always lived up to his adoring fans' expectations, though, and a couple of years ago the mother of a female fan threatened to sue him for allegedly verbally abusing her daughter after refusing to sign an autograph. "I'm a human like everybody else so I make mistakes and I know it," he confides.

He admits there is a tension between trying to satisfy the demands of the fans and trying to live as normal a life as possible. "It's tricky, I can't lie. Sometimes I get lonely. I get depressed on the road just because you feel like the whole of you – mentally, physically and emotionally – has been spent in front of everyone. You feel like you have nothing left for yourself. I have this theory that when you lose it all, that's when you can start again. So when I feel like I've lost my spirit, I sit down and close my eyes and do some meditation. That's when everything starts to flow back into me. It's cool to know that you can bring yourself back to your full life." If you quiz him on the most unusual item he has ever autographed he grins broadly and chuckles "boobs!"

Over the past seven years *NSYNC have spent so much time on the road that they used to have to put Post-it notes backstage to remind them which city they were in. 1997 saw them touring Europe, in 1998 they were back in Europe and in 1999 they began the *NSYNC North America Tour. 2000 saw the start of the sell-out No Strings Attached Tour, followed swiftly by Pop Odyssey in 2001 and culminating with the hugely successful Celebrity Tour in 2002. You can just imagine the state the tour bus used to get in – with five teenage lads and a dog on board (Chris's dog Busta went on tour too)!

"Our tour bus does get in a bit of a mess because we've got Joey in the band," moaned Justin at the time. "He'll drink five bottles of iced tea and toss the bottles on the floor." Joey, though, was at pains to point out that they work well together on and off stage: "We all take it in turns to clean up. We're a pretty diplomatic band." The *NSYNC tour bus was like a mobile hotel. "We've got twelve bunks," said Justin, "so that when our friends and family come out they can stay on the bus too."

His favourite part of the bus was the lounge. "I have to say the back lounge is hot. There are nice couches and a recliner. And there's a ton of candles in the back. I like it when all the lights are out and there's nothing but candles. It's like, whew." There were times when he really needed that time out as the boys were often on the receiving end of threats from jealous teenage lads.

Justin bears no grudges, though, and thinks that insecurity was the main reason behind it. "When we first came out, we got some verbal abuse, but it was just because that's how young American kids fight back from insecurity. I think the group has been accepted into the male audience now. For some reason we're starting to bridge the generation gap too, from younger to older kids to adults."

Despite spending nearly a third of his life living out of a suitcase and away from friends and family, Justin set out on his solo tour of the UK and North America in 2003 in fine form, though he'd be staying in posh hotels this time round. "Whenever we go on tour I get flu the first week – and I mean every time. On one occasion I had a temperature of 102 degrees and I had to have a vitamin B jab because I was so ill," laments Justin. We're sure there are plenty of girls who would love to mop his fevered brow...

The 2003 tour was to be a real departure for Justin because, for the first time ever, he was completely on his own. "I'm looking forward to this tour," he admitted before hitting the road, "because it's the first time I'm touring as a solo artist and the first time I'm getting to perform the songs from *Justified* for my fans." Justin likes to do things properly, so he admitted he'd be putting a lot of pressure on himself to put in a 150% performance. "I'm such a perfectionist. I get really stressed if choreography isn't going well or if I mess up on stage."

Justin has had his fair share of mishaps while touring too. He once broke his thumb by falling over on stage while on tour in Germany. "It was an open-air festival and it was really hot. They were spraying the kids with water with this big hose, and they got some water on the stage. I slid on the water and my feet came out from under me. My first reaction was to throw my hands down – to try to catch myself – and my thumb broke. Luckily it was the last song... I just held the mike in my left hand the whole time."

Fans also nearly caught a flash of Justin's boxers when he was dancing with *NSYNC during a show. "I ran on stage after a quick change with my fly unzipped. My pants almost fell down all the way to my ankles. They fell to my thighs, almost to my knees, and I grabbed them. Luckily I had a baggy basketball shirt on over them, so you couldn't see they fell down." Oops!

On the most recent *NSYNC tour he had a hiccup with his flying harness, as he explains: "We flew above the crowd attached to harnesses. I went up there and got stuck. I didn't come back for several minutes." But he loves the thrill of being on stage and admits he's probably more at ease performing in front of thousands of people than putting on a show for family and friends. "I am more comfortable with 300,000 people at Rock in Rio when we hit the stage, than I am [in an interview].

"It's so funny because the family – whenever we gather round at Christmas or at Thanksgiving or something – is like, 'Get your guitar out and sing something.' And I'm like, 'I don't really feel like it, because there's only about ten people.'" *NSYNC have played some pretty big venues, including the Super Bowl and Rock in Rio. "I think there were about 275,000 people who came to see us. It's pretty incredible when you can't see the end of the crowd."

What does he miss when away from home? "I miss that feeling when you walk into your own house and put your bare feet on the carpet. It's like, 'This is my carpet and I can run around naked if I want!'" We'd let him run around naked on our carpet any time!

Being a hugely successful multi-platinum pop star definitely has its advantages and – luckily for us – Justin is in no hurry to give it all up yet. Every morning when he wakes up, he can't believe how great life is. He says the best thing about being Justin Timberlake is that he is living his dream... and it doesn't get much better than that!

> "I **love the feeling** when you're up there, and the crowd is **getting into** what you're doing. I love to see **smiles on their faces** and know that I had something to do with it!"

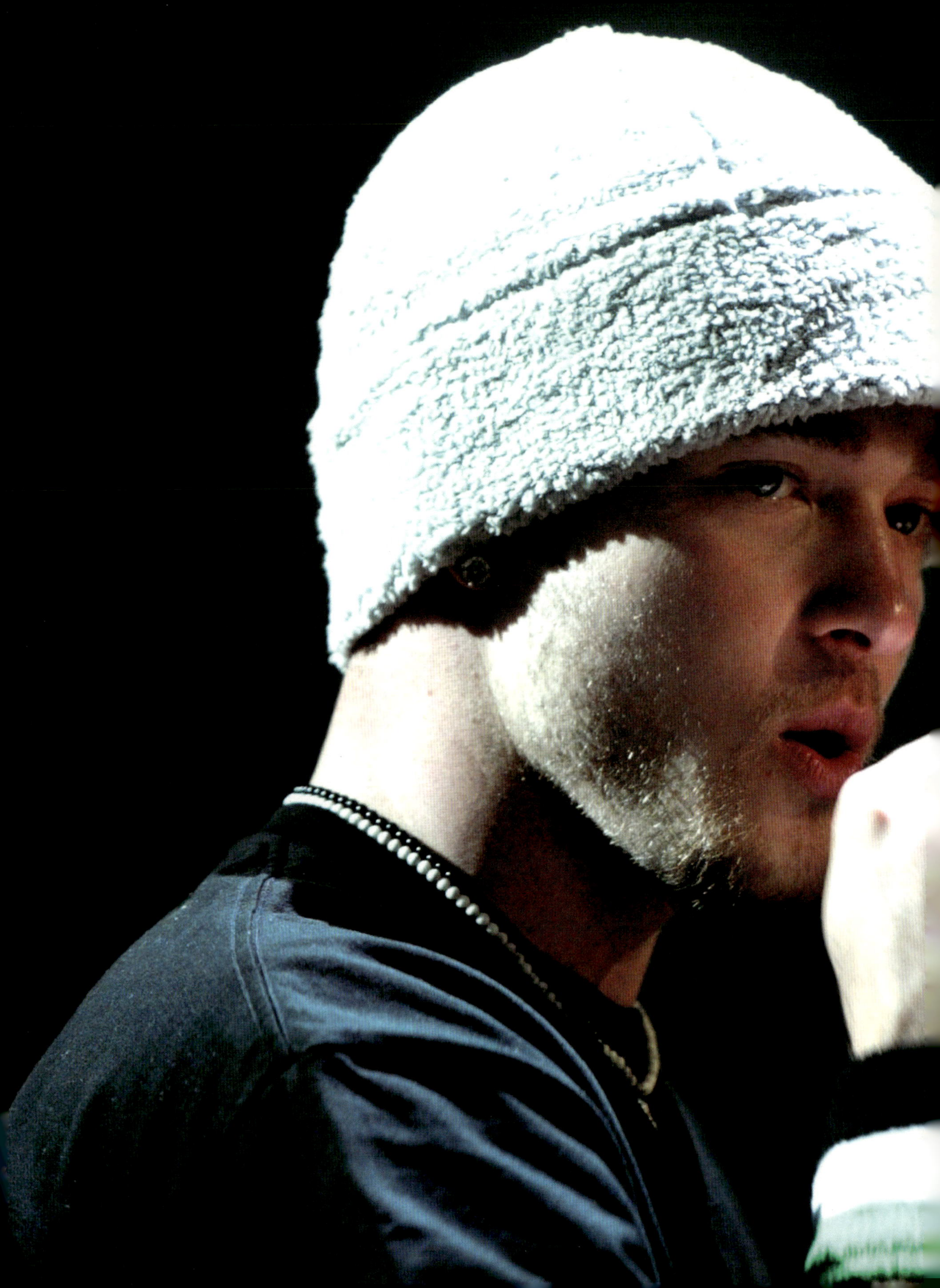

Chapter Five
THE MAKING OF
JUSTIFIED

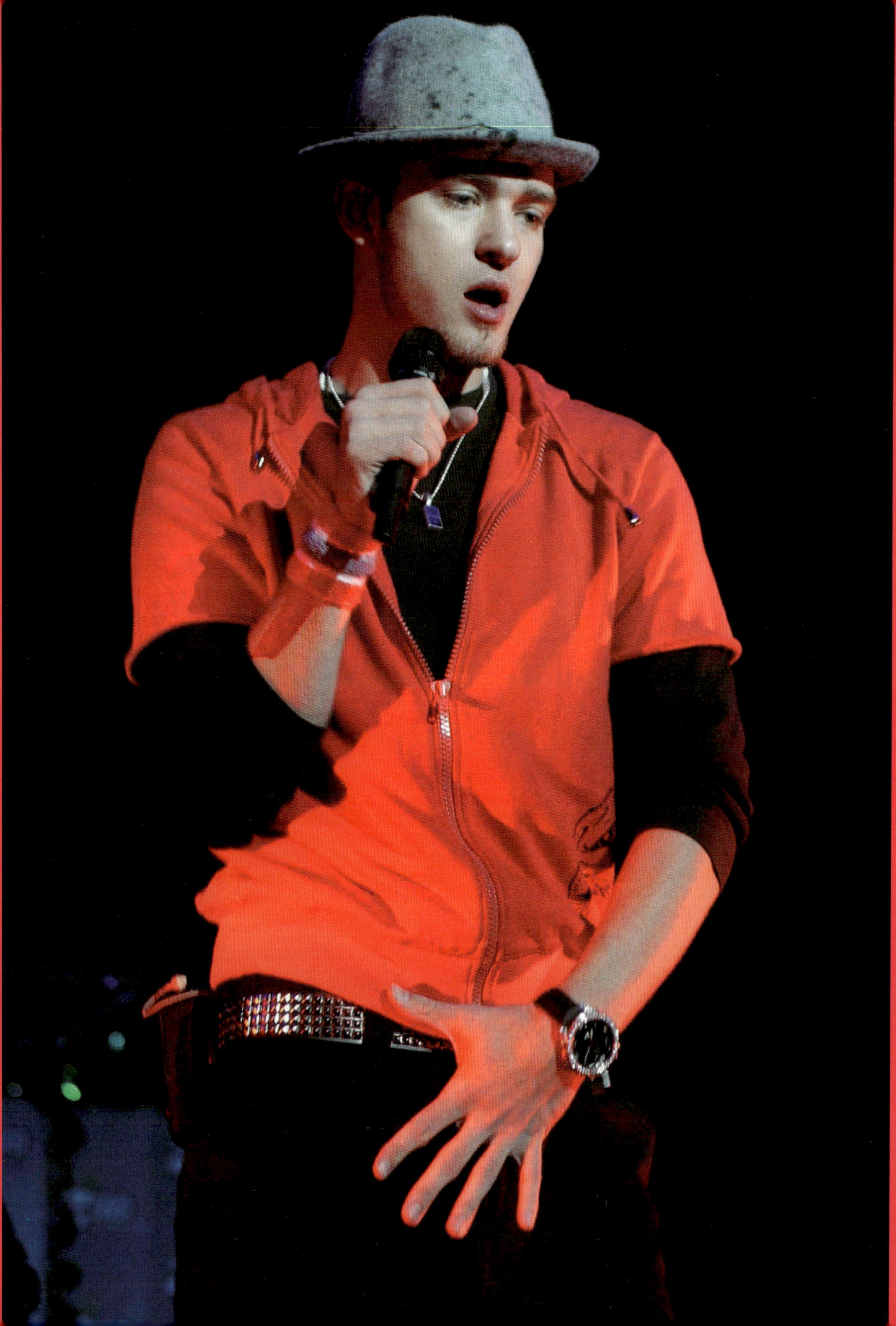

As one fifth of boyband *NSYNC, Justin Timberlake became a household name. His popularity just keeps on growing. He's rich, he's famous and he's doing a job he adores... so why rock the boat and strike out on his own? "My new album is about moving on in life," he explains. "It's been a long-time dream for me. Since I was a little boy all I've wanted to do is make my own record and put it out. That's a hell of a feeling – to wake up and feel so fortunate. I'm getting paid to do what I want to do."

Leaving the shelter of a successful outfit like *NSYNC is a huge risk. Many have trodden the path of fame and fortune as part of a successful band, only to fall at the first hurdle as a solo singer – Gary Barlow, Andrew Ridgeley and Victoria Beckham, to name but three. Robbie Williams may have eclipsed the success of Take That and Diana Ross that of The Supremes, but for the most part going solo can be perilous. Justin, undeterred, felt it was time to break away. "I was in the mood to do my own thing. It wasn't anything personal.

"Aside from *NSYNC, even before we hooked up, this is something that I've wanted since I was little. This is about living out a lifelong dream. *NSYNC had been running for seven years straight and I had so much music inside of me that was so different, it wouldn't be right for anyone else." But how did the other band members react to the news? "I made a conscious decision and told the guys that this is what I wanted to do... this is where my heart was. They were very supportive and I think we were all ready to chill out and take a break."

In making that decision Justin was incredibly brave – some might even say arrogant – but with the phenomenal success of his first solo offering he's forced those critics to eat their words. "I was pleasantly surprised and happy that [the critics] liked the record because they're very hard to please," he says. The album, *Justified*, is nothing like the bubblegum pop of *NSYNC and reveals Justin to be an extremely innovative new talent. "I think if you listen to it it's very urban-sounding and to do that I just did what I thought was me. As an artist that's all you can do," he says simply.

That edgy urban sound comes partly from Justin himself and partly from the prowess of the high-pedigree people he enlisted to help him put the album together. Justin managed to persuade producers like Tim 'Timbaland' Mosely – whose recent credits include Missy Elliott's 'Get Ur Freak On' – and the Neptunes (Chad Hugo and Pharrell Williams), who are producers of Jay-Z and Usher, to get on board, though initially they took some convincing. "At first, I was like, 'He's coming from *NSYNC, I'm coming from my urban world, how we gonna mesh?'" admitted Timbaland. "But when we got together everything was perfect. We worked real good together. It's hard coming from ten million sales to switch styles on your fans and do something different, but he's just being him. I'm down with taking chances cos I'm a chance-taker myself."

One thing that might just have convinced Timbaland to take a chance and produce Justin's first solo album is his uncompromising focus. "It's about specifics. My need for specifics," Justin explains. Working with the Neptunes was easier. "After working with Pharrell and Chad on 'Girlfriend', we had such a connection that it was a no-brainer to work with them again," says Justin. Collaborating with the Neptunes again was like a reuniting of old mates – particularly with Pharrell. "We talk twice a week so, aside from understanding where I want to go as an artist, he understands who I am as a person," reveals Justin. And he's equally enthusiastic about working with Chad again. "He's like a genius to me. He puts these touches on a song that makes it this new creation." The feeling was apparently mutual. "Justin's album is incredible because of the amount of musicality he gave us room to bring to the project," reveals Pharrell. "It's a whole other level."

Justin enjoyed being back in the studio with Timbaland and the Neptunes. "It was a great learning experience for me just to be in the studio with them. The experiences were so different. Pharrell and Chad took a real hands-on approach with writing lyrics and melodies, and Timbaland would come in and say, 'All right, what are we feelin' today?' and put the headphones on. Fifteen minutes later he'd take them off, unplug the sequencer and this crazy-ass beat would come out. I'm blown away every time, because you see him just sit there and punch buttons. He's like, 'You like this beat?' and I'm like, 'You kidding?' So he'd track it and let me do my thing. It was cool to work with different producers and see the different styles."

Justin co-wrote all 13 tracks on *Justified* and says it's an album written straight from the heart. He even gave it its name. "I guess it was just a sense of reckoning for myself. It was so different from what people would expect me to do, so everything about the album has justification for me." He admits he used the musical influences of those people he'd grown up on – like Stevie Wonder, Donny Hathaway, Marvin Gaye, Michael Jackson, Elvis Presley and Al Green – for inspiration. As you listen to each track you can hear brief glimpses of those artists – a staccato Jackson beat, a melodious Wonder harmony and a husky Gaye vocal – among the musical ingredients Justin's cooking with.

Justified gives Timberlake every opportunity to show off his in-depth and well-rounded musical knowledge, coupled with a diverse range of musical tastes. Hip-hop, R&B, rock, soul and country are all used to full advantage, and it shows. "It's not like I set out to create some new sound," he says. "I just wrote what I wanted to hear and drew inspiration from the past. I didn't wanna look back five years from now and regret not trying something different."

Following his instincts turned out to be completely right. It would have been easy to churn out that formulaic sound that made *NSYNC so successful, but it probably wouldn't have been nearly as attractive to all those fans who, like him, have moved on in their musical tastes. "I don't know what some 15-year-old is gonna think about my album," he confesses. "I don't know what a 30-year-old is gonna think about it. But I'll soon know."

In creating *Justified*, he has embarked on a journey through uncharted territory and come out the other side a respected solo artist. Justin's unique blend of hip-hop, R&B and pure soul has won the respect of a new, older, more 'urban' audience – yet he's still managed to retain those *NSYNC fans he matured with. Johnny Wright (who co-manages Timberlake with the singer's mother and stepfather, Lynn and Paul Harless) recognises that "the traditional five-member male pop vocal group is starting to fizzle," and that Justin needed to retain his core teen audience and attract new fans.

"As your musical tastes open up, at some point what you personally like and want to do might not be in the best interest of the group," says Johnny. "So, when you have that passion, you have to step out and present it – and that's what Justin did. All he wanted to do was go out and put some music on CD that was in his heart and get a reaction from fans one way or the other. This is all about the passion and the music that's inside of him."

Writing the album has indeed been an intensely personal experience, its creator confirms. "As a songwriter, the tracks are like your children, you love them all the same. But if I had to pick a favourite it would be 'Nothin' Else'. It's a simple love story, expressing to this ordinary girl how you think she's from another planet."

Recording as a solo artist was a unique experience too. "In *NSYNC you don't do records that somebody doesn't sing on. But with this record I did whatever came to mind. If my voice cracked a little bit, it was character. Leave it on the record. It's totally organic. It's probably the most organic experience I ever had in making music or being creative. It's definitely honest. This album is completely like me."

Track-by-track Justin unveils his amazing vocal range, innovative use of rhythms and personal lyrics. "The lyrics are just the way I say things when I get into those moods that are described in the songs. It's just me on a platter, which is kind of scary," he admits. "The beauty of writing songs is that each one is like a novel, leading me into the next. There's a bit of re-invention every time you come up with a new record."

> "The lyrics are just the way **I say things** when I get into those **moods** that are described on the songs. It's **just me** on a platter which is kind of **scary**."

Of the 13 tracks on the album, the Neptunes produced seven – 'Nothin' Else', 'Senorita', 'Last Night', 'Like I Love You', 'Take It From Here', 'Let's Take A Ride' and 'Rock Your Body' – and Timbaland produced four, including 'Cry Me A River' and '(And She Said) Take Me Now'. The Underdogs produced 'Still On My Brain'. One of Justin's all-time favourite singers, Motown's Brian McKnight, produced romantic balled 'Never Again'. "It was such a great thrill to get to meet Brian when he came to do a guest spot on *MMC*," reveals Justin. "He has the most amazing voice and I admire him so much. He is a very cool guy!"

It is this variety of producers that gives each track a completely different sound – from the Spanish-inflected 'Senorita' to the hip-hop urban sound of 'Cry Me A River'.

Justin is justifiably happy with his solo effort. "I'm just pleased with my album so I feel I have achieved a lot already. I hope other people get enjoyment from it so that I can carry on making the music that I love," he says. He's not the only one either. The critics have been unusually kind to a boy who is better known for his sugar-sweet pop hits as one fifth of *NSYNC. There's one reason why – he's actually proved he's a singer-songwriter worthy of the comparisons that have been made with Michael Jackson. "I was lucky enough to grow up at a time when I could watch Michael and Madonna," he explains. "But on *Justified* I think you'll also hear the Eagles in the harmony and a lot of Stevie Wonder."

He admits that, on the first track, there is a similarity to Michael because of the staccato beats and rhythms, but the rest of the album draws on a vast range of musical inspiration. "As you listen to the album you'll hear some of my stylising coming from where I grew up in Memphis, Tennessee. It's very blues-influenced. I think it's a fusion of other different styles of music," he explains.

"There's other music that's influenced me. I think there are some songs that you'll hear the harmonies and it's more reminiscent of the Bee Gees. And there's a little bit of Queen as well... So you pass to the left, and you sail to the right. Daaah! You know how Freddie used to do that. He was baaaaaaad! He was a baaaaaad mama jama."

When he was making *Justified*, Justin listened to a lot of classic soul and disco. "We drove around in the car listening to old Earth, Wind & Fire albums, and he was totally with it," says Chad Hugo. "The background of those songs is the feeling we wanted to incorporate into the music. He was like, 'Nobody's ever heard anything like that before... a white

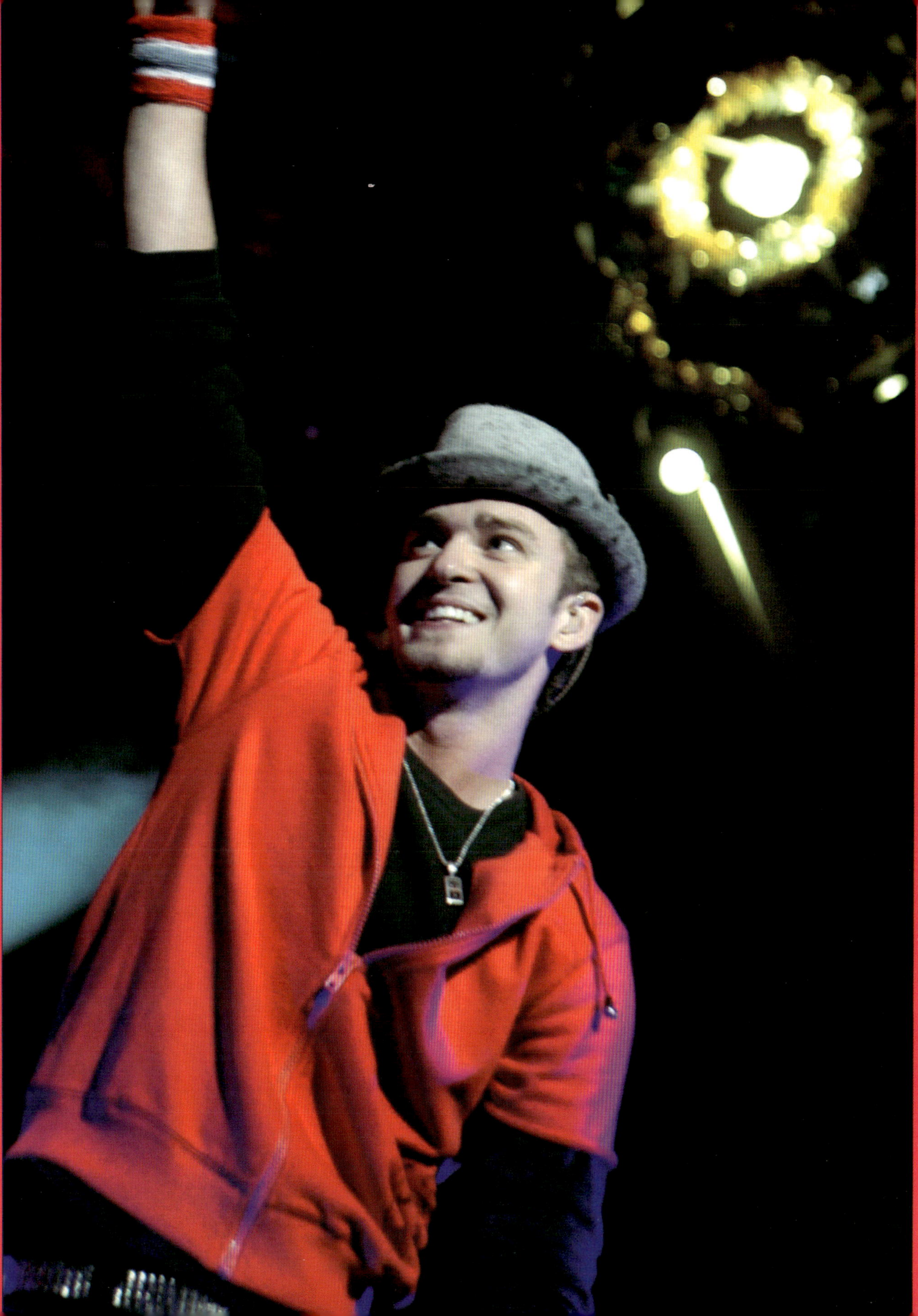

boy singing this kind of music.' He didn't care what people would say." Chad reveals Michael Jackson's music provided inspiration too. "We listened to *Off The Wall* and *Thriller* a bunch of times to really get the feel of them and create something that's not a sample, but similar to those songs without recycling them. We just wanted to re-create that sense of those timeless, classic songs, without any of the 'bling, bling, hit me on my two-way' style of the new R&B."

Justin has always been a big fan of Jacko, all the way up to his latest album. "I did listen to *Invincible* more than once – my favourite song from that record is 'Butterfly'. It's an album that sounds like it took a year to make. I prefer *Off The Wall* because you can hear the rawness in the sound – everything wasn't so rehearsed back then. I like that raw sound of his voice where, if he made a mistake here or there, Quincy [Jones, producer] didn't care. He just kept it and I drew inspiration from those stylised vocals and the recordings. What inspired me was the fact that these songs could be like highly produced demos."

It's a feeling he thinks he captured on *Justified*. "I like how the record feels. You can tell that everybody had a good time making it. There are moments on the record where you'll hear somebody in the background just shout out something and we just kept it on. Like they made records in the old days. We weren't trying to make everything perfect. I think that's the proudest part about the whole thing is that it does sound organic."

Justin enjoyed the solitude of recording the album and found it cathartic. "It was therapeutic. I got some stuff off my chest, I got some ideas down that I wanted to try. So creatively, personally, spiritually, physically, mentally, sexually, it was a very satisfying experience." He admits it was at a time in his life when he needed refuge and creating the music gave him the chance to come to terms with issues in his life. "I went through some real changes while I was making this record," he says.

Justin is surprisingly candid about why he felt as he did. "I was feeling angst in the form of heartbreak, and it was eating me alive. To hear the person who started off and the person who finished, I hear two different people." It seems that the break-up with Britney did play a major part in the making of *Justified*. "Writing a couple of songs on the record helped me to deal with things. I just got better and at the end of the record I was like the person who had just let it all go and said, 'Wow. I'm past this. I'm in a good place.'"

Going solo meant that success or failure rested on Justin's broad shoulders alone. "I kind of feel like everybody has their magnifying glasses out and they're all looking for the pimples now," he says. "Before [if something flopped], I could have obviously just blamed it on Chris," he laughs. "I could have said, 'Yeah, I was in the car, but I wasn't driving.' But now I'm not in the car, I'm on a motorcycle and I'm all by myself." And do the other *NSYNCers approve of the album? "Chris has heard a lot and loves it. They've all been very supportive," says Justin.

His vulnerability is well hidden. Despite, as he says, "feeling a little bit naked" without the boys around him, it's obvious he's having a ball – as his solo performance of 'Like I Love You' at the MTV Video Music Awards showed. As he strode on stage clad in Jacko-esque big brimmed hat and gloves the crowd roared its appreciation. "I had a blast. But I knew I was going to be compared to Michael Jackson. That's a big hat and glove to fill."

His manager Johnny Wright dismisses the criticism that Justin was simply doing a *Stars In Their Eyes*. "In reality, there was no thought about [copying] Michael Jackson. [The idea for] the hat actually came from Frank Sinatra, but nobody even thought about Justin vibing on Frank Sinatra. You can't grow up in the era of Michael Jackson... without having some of that embedded in your soul. But there wasn't a thought in his mind to go out there and try to be Michael Jackson."

Justin denies he was aping those 'Thriller' moves, too. "Anytime someone comes out and dances and does something with choreography, they say, 'Well, that's inspired by Michael.' The responses I've been hearing are that [my performance] was reminiscent of Michael, but at the same time, I did my thing."

But Justin does admit that it was weird being on stage on his own without the other *NSYNC guys. "It's kind of scary being on stage without them but I'm getting used to that – no one to look round at if you forget your moves. I had to realise there were dancers behind me and that they don't have to sing. So, I had to step up my game a lot. Before, if I was slacking slightly I could just say, 'But man, I'm trying to sing!' Now I have to be able to keep up with them. I'm having a good time, though."

Justin believes his biggest challenge in producing his first solo record "was to make sure that it was an honest piece of work, that the songs I did were who I am." We can all agree it's a challenge he's risen to admirably. Manager Johnny Wright says he was excited about the opportunity of working with him on his solo project. "This is not Justin from *NSYNC's solo album. This is Justin Timberlake's first album," he says. "There's a difference. The guy is talented. He's a dope individual. He knows what he likes and he knows what he wants, and he was very easy to work with. I think it's his moment." And so do we.

JUSTIFIED
– THE ALBUM, TRACK BY TRACK

SENORITA
A hot mid-tempo Neptunes number that's more spice than salsa features Hispanic moods coupled with urban undertones. It shows off Justin's very black-sounding vocals that, at times, conjure up a young Stevie Wonder singing the kind of harmonies we heard on *Songs In The Key Of Life*. Pharrell Williams adds credibility with his vocal introduction and urban beats, making this song a pleasure to listen to over and over again.

LIKE I LOVE YOU
Released as a debut single, this is an interesting record to have chosen since it doesn't have the immediate catchiness of a traditional pop single. "I knew it wasn't a first-listen record," explains Justin, "and you'd have to hear it a couple of times

before you got it. But I felt it was the best song to come out with because it sets up the album. It's definitely R&B, it's got the hip-hop element, but at the same time it has a rock flair."

The Neptunes' production stirs, while Justin's vocal arrangement and a hard guitar hook give it its distinctive edge. "Initially people will be surprised to hear my voice in this venue, but I think at the same time people will recognise that it's not contrived at all. I grew up on Stevie Wonder and Marvin Gaye, and Al Green lives down the street from me in Memphis – literally five minutes from me. That's what I grew up on. And hip-hop is what determines pop culture right now."

The high-pitched staccato yelps may be reminiscent of Michael Jackson and the free-flowing rhythms may give you the feeling that you're bang in the middle of a jam session, but together the elements work well to produce a single deserving of the Top Five position it achieved.

(OH NO) WHAT YOU GOT

If you want original this has got to be one of the most interesting tunes on the album. Using a haunting African/Asian influence for the background soundtrack, Justin has produced an inventive rhythmic sound that's a far, far cry from his *NSYNC days. Producer Timbaland works his magic and even joins Justin in the vocals – a dope single for sure!

TAKE IT FROM HERE

With some truly original lyrics, this romantic ballad flows beautifully and is sure to provide some inspirational chat-up lines to lads everywhere. "Girls are going to fall in love with that song," confirms producer Chad Hugo. "It's got this great string section on it, and I think girls should be looking out for some of those pick-up lines. Guys are definitely going to steal some of them!"

"It's basically about how when the whole world is falling apart, I'll be the one who's there to pull you back on your feet," explains Justin. "That is the most genuine way to say 'I love you' to someone." The groove is very loose, a kind of cross between Marvin Gaye and Bill Withers, and Justin has employed the sounds from contemporary artists to get the effect he wanted. "I don't know if people will get this, but the way I treated my vocals in the verse was like Radiohead's Thom Yorke or Coldplay's Chris Martin. It's a soulful track, but I kind of treated the vocals like a rock singer. I fell off the notes, and hoped to make it feel like you're floating when you listen to it." And you do. Justin's vocals are as sweet as honey and lift you high into the clouds. It's the perfect song to close your eyes and chill out to... and at six minutes and 16 seconds playing time it still feels too short!

CRY ME A RIVER

The second single from the album, 'Cry Me A River' was responsible for causing a whole heap of controversy when it was released on video. But more of that later...

Musically, it has that trademark wacky Timbaland beat that makes it stand head and shoulders above the rest of the album. "As soon as Timbaland made that beat, I started humming this crazy melody," says Justin. "I really wanted one section of the song to follow that staccato rhythm, but wanted the other parts to feel like something new." Even if you don't

"Writing a couple of songs on the record **helped me** to deal with things. I just got better and at the end of the record I was like the person who had just **let it all go** and said, '**Wow**. I'm past this. I'm in a **good place**.'"

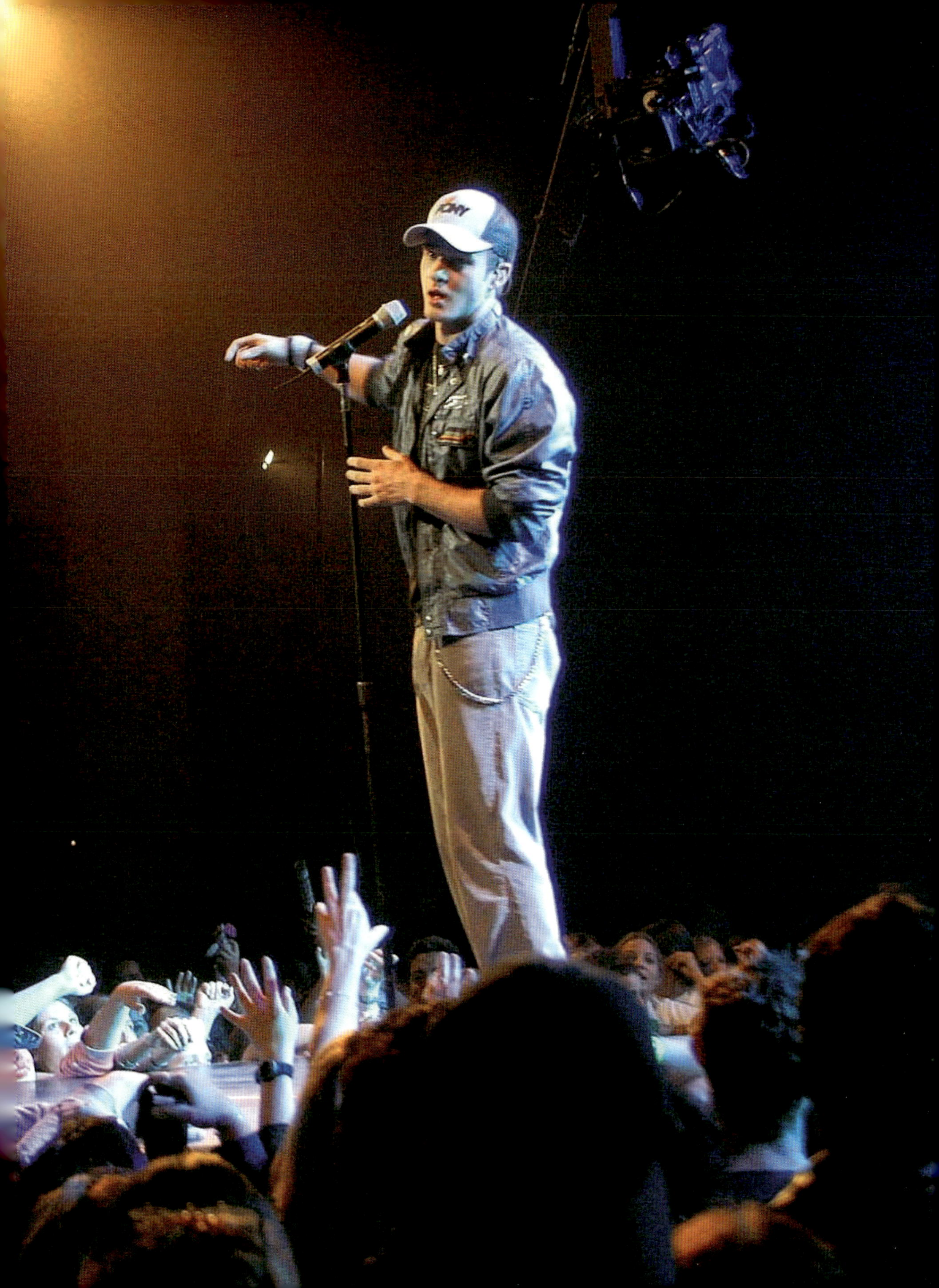

feel the emotion of the song, the groove is undeniable. It was co-produced by hitmaker Scott Storch, of Christina Aguilera's 'Stripped' fame, so it's no surprise this was a hit on both sides of the Atlantic.

But it's the lyrics that have attracted the most attention. It's a haunting tale about a man who's had the dirty done on him but, despite having a broken heart, he refuses to look back. Is Justin referring to his relationship with Britney Spears when he says, "You told me you loved me... now you tell me you need me?" When quizzed whether the lyrics were about the break-up he refused to be drawn. "The song was inspired by the rhythm, and the song was inspired by the way I felt," is all he'll admit. We'll leave you to draw your own conclusions.

ROCK YOUR BODY

With an intro very similar to that of Madonna's 'Holiday', this song is pure 1980s disco complete with those funky, twangy guitar sounds much loved by bands like Earth, Wind & Fire, Kool & The Gang and Mr Jackson himself. R&B beats, a closing beatbox effect and Vanessa Marquis on backing vocals combine to give it meat, while Justin's voice keeps it funky and fresh. Another Neptunes production with lyrics that would make your grandma's hair curl! If there's one track on the album that owes everything to the influence of Michael Jackson, then this is it.

NOTHIN' ELSE

If 'Rock Your Body' is the homage to Michael Jackson, then 'Nothin' Else' is pure respect for Stevie Wonder – right down to the cool electric guitar, accompanying synthesiser and vocal harmonies. This is one of Justin's own favourite tracks, but maybe that's because it reminds him of his childhood musical hero. Timberlake confesses that, when he first met Stevie while laying down tracks for *Celebrity*, he was blown away. "We recorded a ballad that Stevie Wonder played harmonica on. When he came in to record it, that's when I knew I'd made it. I almost cried, just realising that somebody like him is playing on a song I wrote." This is one of the best tracks on the album, for sure.

LAST NIGHT

Featuring those high staccato squeaks so favoured by Michael Jackson in the 1980s, 'Last Night' is a light-hearted dance track from producer Pharrell Williams. It proves Justin can certainly hit those falsetto notes and is one of the reasons Justin is so often compared to Jacko. Lyrically it's hard not to think they are aimed squarely at his ex, right down to the way he abruptly utters those words at the end of the record: "Can't we just get back to that?"

STILL ON MY BRAIN

'Still On My Brain' is a beautiful ballad which demonstrates Justin's musical versatility and vocal ability. Produced by the Underdogs, it has a suggestion of Stevie Wonder in the vocal arrangement – piano backing, bells and 45 rpm vinyl crackle, and it takes you right back to that Motown sound of the 1960s. Vocally Justin is more reminiscent of a young Michael Jackson. A classic disco slowie to snog the night away to.

(AND SHE SAID) TAKE ME NOW

Producer Timbaland has come up with a number that Marvin Gaye would have been proud of, right down to Janet Jackson's husky backing vocals. Who'd have thought that nice-boy Justin could come up with something quite so naughty? If any record proves he's left his boyband straitjacket behind and slipped into something a little more comfortable, 'Take Me Now' is it! "I think it's a really sexy record. A lot of it's about sex, but it's done in a genuine way. There were actually things we had to tone down a little bit," Justin reveals. "I think sex is beautiful." We want to hear the unedited version!

RIGHT FOR ME

This raunchy, fast-paced number produced by Timbaland is a departure from the style of the rest of the album. Featuring rapper Bubba Sparxxx, it uses a mixture of finger-clicking and humming samples which combine with Justin's vocals to produce an original sound that never gets boring. It has a hypnotic resonance that keeps you entranced – and the lyrics are very saucy, too... though Justin says we shouldn't read too much into them. "Songs are songs. I don't think too much about the lyrics, they just come to me. It's fun." Seems Justin just gets steamier as the album progresses!

LET'S TAKE A RIDE

Just when you thought you could predict what was coming next, Justin and his production pals the Neptunes surprise you again. A fast-paced effort that urges you to just pull down the hood, turn on the car stereo and drive... We love it!

NEVER AGAIN

Brian McKnight produced this love song, an exceptionally beautiful ballad that really displays Justin's vocal ability. Lyrics hang heavy with poignancy and regret, while Justin's soft tones immerse each word in sadness and despair as he exhibits a truly remarkable vocal range. His voice is strong enough to carry the song with only a light guitar and keyboard accompaniment. In a word, smoochy.

WORTHY OF

For a bonus track this is really rather good. The beat is easy and catchy and Justin's vocals sweep you along with that chillin' vibe. Soul to sway to. And yes, Justin, you are a man that can keep us happy if you keep making music like this!

> "I think it's a really **sexy record**. A lot of it's about **sex**, but it's done in a genuine way. There were actually things we had to **tone down** a little bit."

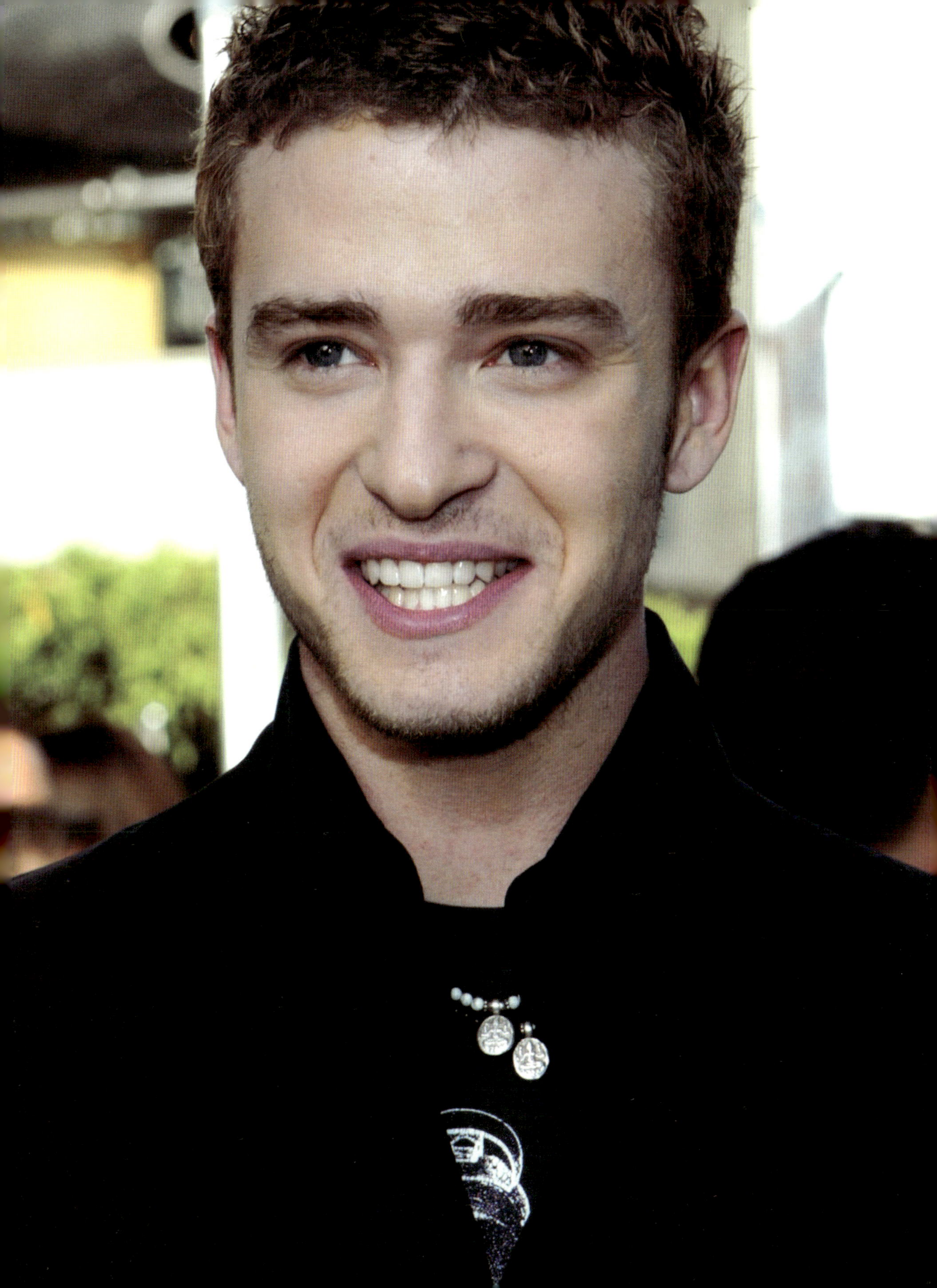

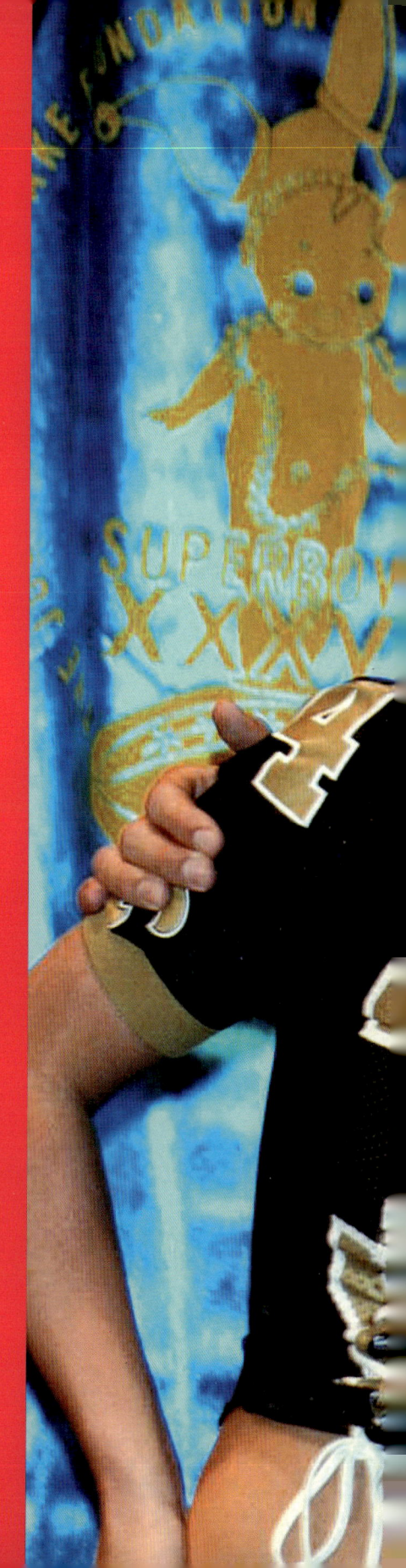

Chapter Six
JUSTIN LOVES BRITNEY

"I'm a **hopeless romantic**... when I fall for somebody, **I fall hard**. It takes a lot for me to fall for someone, but when I do, that's when **I give them everything**."

It's not hard to see why Justin Timberlake was named one of America's top 50 bachelors in *People* magazine and voted Favourite Male Sex Symbol and Favourite Male Performer in *Teen Beat*. He's certainly got the looks – dazzling azure eyes, thick blond hair and a bronzed body that's guaranteed to get a girl's pulse racing and the boys running straight to the gym.

Then there's the money that buys diamond-studded watches and top-of-the-range sports cars. The $5 million home earned by album sales that, together as a solo and band artist, total over 35 million. The talent – an achingly beautiful voice, raw, grinding dance moves and the ability to pen songs that are so hip they make you want to move, so soulful they make you want to cry.

But above all that, Justin is one of those rare men who believes in love, romance and all that slushy stuff that women adore. He's also a one-woman type of guy and describes himself as a loyal boyfriend. "I'm a hopeless romantic... when I fall for somebody, I fall hard. It takes a lot for me to fall for someone, but when I do, that's when I give them everything."

Ever since he was thrust into the limelight, Justin has been a magnet for thousands of female fans desperate to get close to him. Not that he claims to understand why. "I don't know how I turned into a 'sex god'," he smilingly protests, admitting that, "All the girls are after a piece of my big old American Pie." To accusations that he is the perfect male specimen, he just says: "To me, perfection is somebody who is completely comfortable with all their imperfections." Modest or not, for millions of teenage girls Justin is hot stuff and by far the tastiest dish in *NSYNC.

But it wouldn't be long before he would be snatched up by pop diva Britney Spears, whom he met on the set of the *Mickey Mouse Club* when he was only 12. It wasn't until a few years later in March 1999 that they finally got it together. "We met up again at a radio station roadshow and kinda hung out," recalls Justin. "On our first date we went out for dinner in Los Angeles."

"We talked and ate all night. It was cool," remembers ex-squeeze Britney. In those days she was very shy and remembers her beau having loads of admirers. "He's very attractive." We've noticed!

For a couple of years the pair tried to keep their relationship under wraps, but it wasn't long before the news was out and the couple's romance became the most highly publicised in history – since Posh and Becks, that is! It was "the real thing" as far as Justin and Britney were concerned, and each thought they had found their perfect partner. "Britney is kind, thoughtful, sensitive, caring, romantic, easy-going and generous," said Justin. Phew, is that all? Britney felt the same. "He's really romantic, caring, loving and generally a really wonderful person," she gushed. Justin was the perfect boyfriend, leaving romantic notes on Britney's pillow or in her bag and sending her flowers when they were apart. "I believe it's the small things that make a difference," he advocated.

Although their both being pop stars meant that they could understand the pressures each was under, it also meant that the two lovebirds often spent a great deal of time apart. "If anybody understands anything I'm going through, it's her, " enthused Justin when they were deeply in love. "And she knows that I can understand anything she's going through because I'm on that end of the spectrum with her. Some people think our schedules make it harder for us, but in a lot of ways, mentally and emotionally, our careers make it easier because we understand each other."

Justin had dated people who were not in the business, "and they just did not understand my life. On top of that, I think I've scored with her being just a wonderful person. I don't know anyone else in this world who has as big a heart as she does. That's the greatest thing about her. Even when she doesn't understand, she understands that she doesn't understand, because she has such a big heart."

They were pop's perfect couple, despite tabloid speculation on Britney's virtue after she famously declared herself a virgin – and, by association, Justin was too. "I want sex just like any other 19-year-old girl does, but I want to have it in a committed marriage," she insisted. "We both plan to stay virgins until we get married. It's tough to resist the temptation but we're determined to keep ourselves pure until the wedding night." Luckily for teen queen Brits, Justin apparently felt the same. "I am probably the only guy my age now who's a virgin and that's OK with me. I don't feel the need to prove my manhood by jumping into bed with every girl that comes along.

"When the group is touring," he continued, "the opportunity comes up all the time. But that's not the kind of relationship I'm looking for. I want to marry a girl who has the same values as I have." But poor old Justin must have found it hard keeping his feelings in check when Britney swapped the pigtails for belly-piercings and cropped skirts!

While Timberlake kept relatively quiet, Britney, it seemed,

"I want to **marry** a girl who has the **same values** as I have."

wouldn't stop banging on about their whiter-than-white relationship. "Justin and I are very lucky to have found each other. We share the same values and he totally understands that I have really strong morals, and that just because I look sexy it doesn't mean I'm a naughty girl!"

But when asked in a leading pop magazine a couple of years later whether they were committed to staying virgins until they were married, both were evasive in their replies. "I still have very strong beliefs," said Britney, while Justin would only offer, "We are committed to each other – and that's all that matters."

Like any relationship, the stars had their fair share of ups and downs. Rumours abounded that the couple had briefly split when Britney turned up to her 18th birthday bash with Robbie Carrico of US teen band Boyz N Girlz United. It's more likely Robbie was simply there as a decoy to get the press off the scent that Justin and Britney really were serious about each other. When Justin forked out an estimated $10,000 for a Cartier ring for his dream girl to match his own, the tabloids went wild. Speculation mounted that the couple were getting engaged, but Justin and Britney at that stage still insisted that they were just good mates who enjoyed hanging out together.

Finally, in 2000, the couple came clean and admitted they were deeply 'in lurve'. It wasn't your normal love affair, though – there was no chance of a romantic candlelit dinner for two at a local Italian restaurant if three minders, 30 paparazzi and 300 fans had anything to do with it! And the pair still spent far more time apart than together. "We speak on the phone about four or five times a day when we're away," admitted Justin. "Can you imagine my phone bill when I was in Australia?" said Britney. "It cost more than my suite. It's crazy." When they did spend time together it was usually just chilling out, listening to music. "When we have time together we prefer to stay in and enjoy our privacy," said Britney in happier times.

It seemed that theirs was a love affair that would last forever and they both had plans to spend the rest of their lives together. "We'd both like to have children – I've always wanted a big family. A whole basketball team would be good," joked Justin. Britney was even thinking about wedding bells. "I want a small outdoor wedding with just close friends and family. It will be very special," she said.

In the summer of 2000, when Justin was spotted whipping out a £30,000 ring over coffee in New York, it seemed like the fairytale would at last have a happy ending. "I want to spend the rest of my life with him," gushed Britney. "I want to grow old with him. We are going to get married and we've been thinking about next year but it depends on our schedules," she admitted.

But it wasn't long before the cracks began to appear and the rumour mill started to roll. Justin and Britney were in the spotlight and their relationship was splashed all over the tabloids. Just why was Justin snapped in the back of a cab with sexy ex-All Saint Nicole Appleton? And did Britney have a romantic dinner with Lee from Steps? Who knows whether the naughty pair were playing away from home or just having a good night out with other pop mates? They both vehemently denied a rift. "I don't know who started the rumour," said Britney. "We never split. That would be too painful. We are soul mates." Indeed, she described Justin as "perfect" and vowed they would be together forever.

As 2001 turned into 2002 more stories surfaced in the papers – was Britney really acting when she stripped down to her underwear and snogged sexy co-star Anson Mount in the filming of *Crossroads*, and did Justin try to get his own back by engaging in some tonsil-tickling with a good-looking brunette in the video for *NSYNC's 'Gone' single? Who knows? Since the couple still appeared to be firmly together it amounted to no more that scurrilous tittle-tattle… until the bombshell dropped in March 2002.

Just as Justin's career was about to take off the couple announced they had split, but maintained it was amicable and they had simply grown apart because of their hectic schedules. But of course the rumour-mongering didn't end there. Before the month was out, front-page stories in the tabloids alleged that pop princess Britney wasn't nearly as squeaky-clean as she liked to make out. It was claimed that Justin had spilled the beans to a fellow passenger on a flight from Atlanta to LA. Stories circulated that Justin had sniped: "Everyone thinks she's a virgin but that's a joke. She lost her virginity a while ago – I should know." The supposed "king of kiss and tell" then reportedly went on to reveal the real reason why they'd split. "We split up because she wanted to get married and I didn't. We're too young to think about that, but she was driving me crazy about it."

The release of 'Cry Me A River' later that year told a very different story, however. The lyrics seemed to imply that Britney had cheated on him, with Justin angrily addressing his former love with lines like, "The damage is done… Tonight I don't think I'll spare your feelings."

When quizzed about who the song was aimed at, Justin was keeping tight-lipped. "I'm not going to specifically say if any song is about anybody," he insisted. "I will say writing a couple of songs on the record helped me deal with a couple of things. To me, songs are songs. They can stem from things that completely happened to you personally, or they can stem from ideas you think could happen to you."

Nobody could escape the fact that the video appeared to be a direct shot at his ex-love, and it is difficult to separate the fact from fiction. Fiction: Girl (played by model/actress Lauren Hastings) sporting newsboy cap, pink-tinted sunglasses and fairy tattoo on lower back cheats on

> "We split up because she **wanted** to get married and **I didn't**. We're too young to think about that, but she was driving me **crazy** about it."

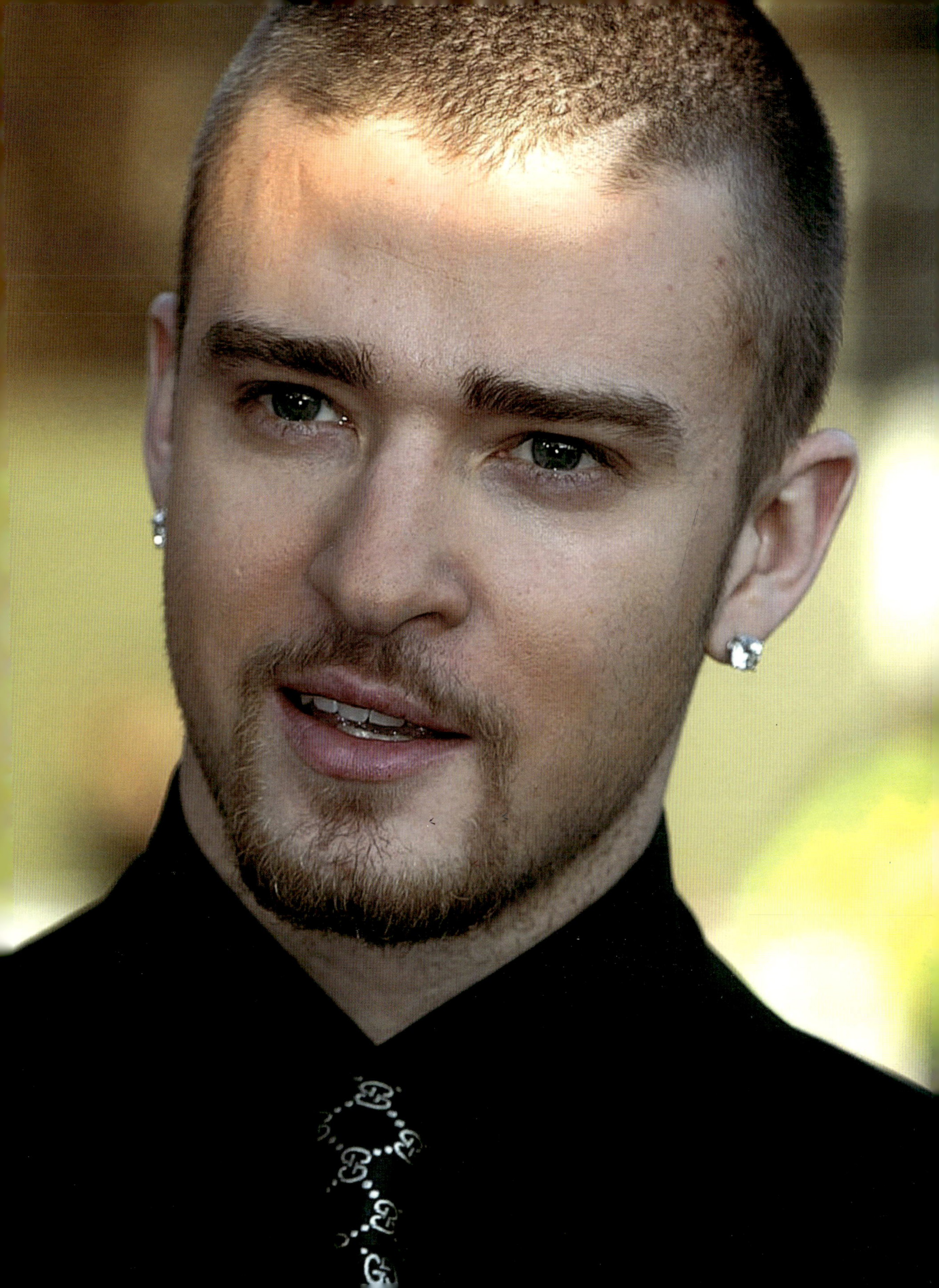

"**No one** knows what went on between Britney and me **except us**. I was **never** unfaithful."

boyfriend and drives off in smart sports car. Boy, played by Justin, breaks into apartment, makes out with a saucy-looking brunette and leaves a video of the evidence to get even. Fact: Britney favours newsboy caps, tinted sunglasses and has a fairy tattooed on her back. She also drives a Porsche Boxster and Lauren Hastings looks uncannily like the teen pop queen. Justin was dating sexy ex-*Melrose Place* actress Alyssa Milano at the time... and she just happens to have brown tresses.

Could it really be just fabrication? Justin says so. "The video is not about her. The video is about me." He claims the idea came from director Francis Lawrence and that they produced it so everyone would talk about it – no bad thing when you want to draw attention to the fact you've got a new single out. "I knew what I was doing," he says. "When you become a product of the media's rumour mill you kinda get this 'thing' about you. It was a chance for me to use it and do a little reversing. To go, 'Now, I've got all of you in the palm of my hand.'"

Britney wasn't giving anything away either, refusing to comment on the video except to say, "The last time I looked in the mirror, I didn't think I really looked like her," and "Boys will be boys." Theories on who Britney had done the dirty on Justin with were rife – *NSYNC choreographer Wade Robson was the hot favourite, though he denies any romantic involvement. Other contenders for the crown of love rat were Prince William (Britters has always had a soft spot for Wills), Ben Affleck (whom she once described as "really hot") and Britain's own Hugh Grant (he, apparently, is rather smitten with Ms Spears and she thinks "he's cute"), but nothing' stuck.

Whatever the reason, the split hasn't been easy for Justin to cope with. "The break-up was absolutely heartbreaking for me. Heartbreak ate me alive." It seems it's not the first time he's been badly hurt. "I've had my heart broken plenty of times." He has his own theory on what mends a broken heart. "It's like being drunk. Nothing helps except time. They used to teach us that in school. When you get drunk, some say a cold shower helps, some say a coffee helps, but nothing helps except time." His mum has helped him bear the pain and try to move on with his life. "When he calls and says his heart is broken, we try to console him," says ever-supportive Lynn.

He's such a nice guy that he even has sympathy for how Britney must have felt. "I'm sure the whole thing was really painful for her, too. But I still have so much love for her as a person, and we still talk every once in a while. Her family was like my family. I recently ran into her mother and sister, and I love them." Britney was also devastated. "The break-up was horrible. Very upsetting and it took a lot out of me," she confessed. "He was my first real love and I doubt I'll be able to love anyone like that again."

So why did they split up? Nearly a year after the four-year romance crumbled the world is still left wondering. "Everyone was interested," says Justin's grandma Bobbye Timberlake, "even people my age. I think it's just because they were like the little bride and groom on top of the wedding cake, a little Ken and Barbie." Justin has said little about why they split. "No one knows what went on between Britney and me except us. I was never unfaithful."

Despite their big bust-up and all the press speculation, Justin remains on speaking terms with his former love. "We're still friends. If we part ways on our terms it's nobody else's business," he says. "I fell in love with Britney. I've known her since I was 12. I can't sit here and say that she's been a dark part of my life. She's been a big sunshine in my life. I've learned so many things."

He insists that there's no way they wouldn't continue to stay friends. "Her family has been part of my family. I also believe... and this is not a prediction... but we are both young. Who knows what's going to happen?" Indeed, at the beginning of 2003 it even looked like the couple were going to give it another go as the pop princess was seen arriving at her ex-love's mansion and was also invited to Justin's 22nd birthday bash in LA. But nothing came of the speculation. "If I thought we should be together, I would be with her. It's as simple as that. And that's all I'm willing to say about it without it getting too personal," says Justin.

He says he is trying to move on with his life. "I can't let go. It's my biggest struggle and I know it's a lesson I am going to have to learn in this lifetime – how to let go. I hope no one goes through what I went through. They say that before you can know love you have to know the opposite so... I don't know. That's the toughest thing I've ever gone through." Ultimately, he feels the timing was wrong. "When we were together it was bliss, like something from a fairy tale. I may not ever get over her. That's why I'm kinda chillin'. I'm waiting to see... but I have to realise that I may never get over her."

With a reconciliation looking unlikely, Britney didn't waste any time rushing into the arms of another man. First she was seen cuddling up to *Titanic* actor Leonardo DiCaprio at the Playboy Mansion. "He looks hot these days," she apparently told one interviewer. Then she was linked with Limp Bizkit frontman Fred Durst, who declared he'd "never felt this way about anyone before"; next she was seen out on the town with playboy actor Colin Farrell, whose bedroom antics are as legendary as Britney's virtue! Other supposed love links included dancer Brian Friedman and Swedish model Marcus Schenkenberg.

Now Justin is young, free and single again, is he on the lookout for a new woman in his life? "I feel like I can look and really figure out [what I want]. I have this whole theory on dating. You know how you go on a job interview and you meet the secretary and she's sweet and looks like she's having such a good time doing what she's doing? And then you finally get in to meet the boss and he's an ass... I feel like [with dating], you go through about four to six weeks of the secretary, then you meet the boss." He's got his own theories on kissing, too. "A kiss shouldn't come from the mouth. A kiss should come from the heart.

"Sometimes they're a little too wet – but I like them in their imperfections, because they're genuine. When a kiss comes from the heart, you can feel it. That's what I do when I kiss. I kiss people with my soul. I don't kiss people with my mouth." Justin described his first kiss, which was when he was 13 and with a girl called Mindy at a birthday party, as "wet, long and beautiful".

If you believe what you read in the press, the footloose Justin is making the most of his new-found single status.

He's been linked with a bevy of beauties, most notably with Britney's arch-rival Christina Aguilera and dance queen Janet Jackson. He describes Christina as looking desirable, but he hasn't confessed to any involvement other than professional. "She does look very hot, doesn't she? She's not calling it wrong – she does look dirty."

When asked if he and Janet were together, he replied: "I love Janet to death. I know her very well. She's a sweetheart. *NSYNC opened for her when she did the Velvet Rope Tour. I've always been linked [romantically] to so many different people, and it's retarded. I know Janet, she knows me. We're friends, and there's nothing in the world that would change our friendship."

Justin's relationship with Alyssa Milano, whom he'd met in a trendy Los Angeles bar, obviously got up somebody's nose. Was it really a coincidence that Britney was seen sporting a T-shirt emblazoned with the words "Dump Him!" while Justin was stepping out with the raven-haired actress? By February 2003, though, the "affair" had calmed down. "It's still a fresh thing," said Justin, "and if I had to say I'd say we were friends."

There were also tales of dalliances with *NSYNC backup dancer Jenna Dewan, but Justin is keeping it buttoned. "She's a friend. I'm not going to talk about it. I want to get to know that person before the whole world tries to get to know us. If they see me with someone else, they are going to think 'playboy.' I have always been a one-woman type of guy." Though if the latest stories are true, he's had flings with not one but both the Minogue sisters!

Women just can't resist Mr Timberlake's obvious charms... but what is it about a woman that turns him on? "Pretty is cool, but it's not really about looks for me. It's more about personality. I like a girl with a good sense of humour, who's humble and sensitive." He likes girls who are understanding and sweet, but he really hates moody females. "Something that women should know is that no, no, no, hell no, we cannot read your minds. I don't get how women say something that means something else, like 'I'm not going to get upset.' You have to think twice, because they probably will get upset. When I say something... I mean it."

And what is the first thing he looks for in a girl? "The first thing I look for in a girl is her mouth, but, as far as body parts go, I'm a butt guy. I like some junk in the trunk," he says cheekily. "I'm a butt man! I like the way the small of a woman's back forms a nice onion."

Justin reckons personality is the most important thing, though, and he likes girls who aren't afraid to go for it. "Someone that lives life to the fullest. Be your own person. I think the main thing about teenage romance is that people try to get to know somebody else before they really know themselves and they end up with a whole other personality that's not them."

Justin sees confidence as an extremely attractive trait. "Not overwhelming, not sassy stuck-up types, but someone who knows themselves and is comfortable with themselves." He adds, "I don't think I have a particular taste in females as far as looks go. If I catch a vibe off somebody and I relate to them... then I feel an attraction."

> "Pretty is **cool**, but it's not really about looks for me. It's more about **personality**. I like a girl with a good sense of **humour**, who's humble and **sensitive**."

He thinks he is a good judge of character. "If someone has a good character then everything kind of goes from there. This means they need to be trustworthy, honest, open." Our Justin knows what turns him off too. He doesn't like insecurity. "I think so many things stem from insecurity... like jealousy for example." So his ideal girl would have to have... "a sense of humour. But she has to be intelligent. I want to be able to talk to her. I guess I want an all-over picture. Everyone deserves the best and everyone has somebody out there for them."

So if female readers are wondering the best way to hook Justin, it's simply to be yourself and have the courage to go for it. "Confidence is sexy," he reveals. "If you come up and start talking to me, you're gonna turn my head. It takes a lot to turn my head and that's something that really does. You start dating someone and you start acting like someone you're not and that's because you probably don't know yourself yet. I know that the first impression I give off is a little intimidating."

He admits that he doesn't talk that much when he meets people. "I'm kinda quiet and reserved and I study people when I first meet them. They might think 'he doesn't talk too much and he's rude', but it's really that I want to study people before I start conversing with them. The fact that somebody can start talking to me and be comfortable with themselves and not worry about anything else, that turns me on." He, on the other hand, isn't always so confident with the opposite sex. "I'm not an upfront type of person with girls – I'm kinda shy."

His idea of a perfect date is simple enough. "Being at home, relaxing with candles. Talking and listening to music – anything old like Stevie Wonder, Marvin Gaye, Al Green." He says all a girl has to do to get him interested is "Get to know me, take the time. I think a girl should do something that a guy would do – surprise me like a guy would. Show up and take me out to dinner, take me somewhere. You often hear about a guy doing that – but, when a girl does that, it's attractive! To do something like that really shows self-confidence." He, on the other hand, also likes to surprise people. "I'd show up and just take somebody out to a nice restaurant, or bungee jumping, or something. I like the element of surprise. I think it's extra special."

Lately Justin seems to prefer partying the night away in various clubs. "I don't necessarily know if I have a bad-boy image," he says, but admits he has "a definite dark side. I think a lot of artists have that... a lot of people who are creative have. I mean, obviously you see a bit of it in the video for 'Cry Me A River'. I dunno, I just think I have this dark side to me." More recently he's admitted to being an animal in bed and says sex has never been taboo for him. "I enjoy it and I praise it and I embrace it and I celebrate it – openly, fun-ly and freely."

He has a growing number of thirty-something female fans but is confident there is nothing they could teach him about sex that he doesn't know already. "I've been doing this since I was 15," he says smiling. "I am very expressive sexually." You might think this runs contrary to his earlier insistence that he and Britney were saving themselves for each other – but we suspect Justin finds playing games with the press almost as much fun as with the opposite sex!

Physically, Justin has always been attractive to the ladies, and in poster-boy terms was by far the most popular of the *NSYNCers. From a young teenager of only 14, his mass of blond curls and big blue eyes made him a real babe magnet. Age has transformed Justin into a tall (he's over 6ft 1in), muscular (he weighs 170lbs) young man. His six-pack is much admired, so much so that he's just won the contract to advertise trendy US gym Bally Total Fitness for a reputed six-figure sum. (The TV ad features hunky Justin performing his single 'Rock Your Body' while men and women work out around him.)

Justin may have had his heart broken but he still believes in the possibility of marriage. "If it comes along and you're in love with someone, that's when you know. But until then, we're all searching. I think when you meet that certain person you'll know it." And he has his own theories on relationships and what makes them succeed. "Every relationship takes some working but when it's going good everything seems perfect," he says.

Justin values trust above all else because without trust, he says, a relationship just can't work. "If you love someone as much as you possibly can and you don't trust that person, it's never going to work. And if you don't communicate with that person from the beginning, they can never trust you." Perhaps it's the experience of his mum and dad's failed marriage that has made Justin believe trust is a crucial element in any relationship. He continues, "Love is the basis of everything. You start to have chemistry with someone, and then you fall in love. Love is about personality. Cute girls obviously catch the eye, but you need to know someone before you fall in love."

He also says that communication is important but admits it can be hard keeping things going when he's on the road performing. "You should communicate exactly how you feel. You also have to be really humble and realise when you've made a mistake."

He has had his fair share of heartache, from witnessing his parents' painful divorce at a young age to being two-timed by girls he dated in his teens. "I think there's a lot of give and take that needs to happen. I've been cheated on numerous times by ex-girlfriends. It's hard for me to trust somebody."

Justin reckons the reason he used to get his heart broken so often is because he was too nice. "I can never find an honest woman! Every woman I've met in the past has been dishonest to me and it's made me wary of relationships." He also believes he has scared some people away. "I can't have meaningless relationships with women. I have to find Miss Right in order to have a relationship. There has to be that big moment when she comes along..."

Despite the disappointments, one thing is for sure: Justin Timberlake is still the sexiest man in pop – and what's more, he's single. Any regrets? "I don't regret anything. Single life is something you have to get used to. I've been asked the question 'How is it going to feel to see [Britney] with somebody else?' so many times. Answer is, it's going to hurt."

Justin has a philosophical view on love and heartbreak. "I think to really experience love, you have to be open to complete and utter devastation and destruction. I'm a

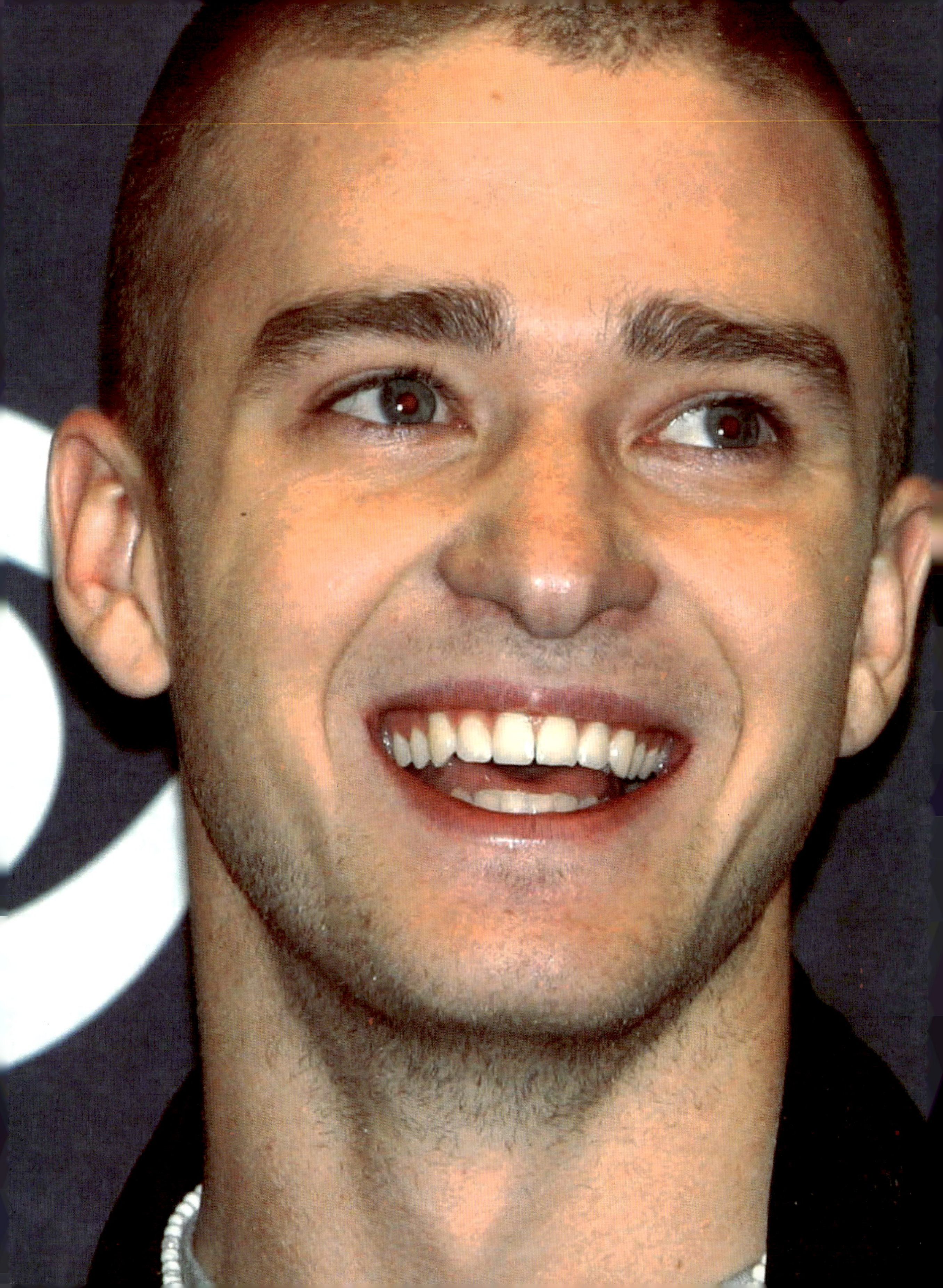

"I think to really **experience love**, you have to be open to complete and **utter devastation** and destruction. I'm a dreamer, **I'm a romantic.**"

dreamer, I'm a romantic." He doesn't pretend that being single is all good fun, either. "Days will go by when I miss... I miss the good things. Britney always surprised me. She has a big heart, a really big heart. That always impressed me."

Despite these occasional moments of sadness, Justin still likes to spend time with the fairer sex. He explains, "I'm new to the whole dating thing. It's very weird. But I don't want a girlfriend." He says he has spent so long in lengthy relationships (four years with Britney) that he's currently relishing his independence. Yet reports in the British press suggest that the dust hasn't yet settled on that relationship. Months after the big bust-up, the pair were spotted sharing an intimate drink together at the White Lotus nightclub in Hollywood. Reports said they appeared to be getting along well and, after two hours of close conversation, left together with their respective entourage of bouncers and drove off in the direction of Britney's house.

A close friend of the teen queen reckons the pair split because Britney cheated on JT, but adds that she now regrets it more than anything and is desperate to get back with him. Will Justin relent and take her back? Well, in her favour is the memory of the most romantic thing a woman has ever done for him. "Britney surprised me for my birthday and took me away to this remote Caribbean island. We stayed for a week, and it was cool. It was spiritual. We felt like there was nobody else on earth. It definitely had a *Blue Lagoon* vibe to it."

A permanent reconciliation remains unlikely, though, because Justin finds it difficult to forgive and forget. "You know what I'm really crap at?" he says. "Forgiveness. Because my perfectionism in my craft sometimes carries over into all areas of my life. There were times when my mom would upset me, and it would take me forever to get over it."

Stories in the press suggested that Justin's family was pleased to see him split from his pop pal. His grandma Sadie Bomar said Britney was a distraction from his music and that now he can concentrate on his career. Ironically, history shows there may be some truth in that. Since splitting with Britney, Justin has produced his first album and made his mark on Planet Pop as one of the most innovative and original solo artists of the moment. Nobody will ever know for sure whether this would still have been the case if he hadn't called it quits with Ms Spears. The break-up may have had a silver lining after all, in that it allowed him to step out from under Britney's shadow and become Justin the pop star instead of simply Britney's boyfriend.

Timberlake has sometimes let a hint of bitterness surface. In one recent interview he said: "Women are spiteful. They know how to push our buttons because they are so much smarter than us. They act like they are not controlling you." In his eyes nobody will ever match up to his mum. "You keep searching for someone as good as your mother... and that's a losing battle."

Despite this, Justin says that if he had to choose between love, money and fame he would always choose love. And if he were to fall in love again, who does he think his mum would prefer to see him with? "She doesn't care. She just wants me to be happy." And what makes him happiest in life? "I enjoy music, man. It really does make me happy."

Though he says he doesn't want a girlfriend right now, arguing that "it's pointless looking for love" and "music is my love at the moment," our bet is it won't be long before he gets snapped up. Reports at the time of writing made film star Cameron Diaz a hot favourite. But anyone hoping the lovelorn superstar may choose them as his future mate will have to be patient... and perfect!

"I haven't yet found this girl I keep writing about," Justin admits. But hope springs eternal. "I think someday, I really will meet my angel. She doesn't have a distinct face, just a presence. She just glows." He may not have found his perfect partner yet – but luckily for 22-year-old Justin, he's got plenty of time to have fun looking!

Chapter Seven
JUSTIN IN BRITAIN

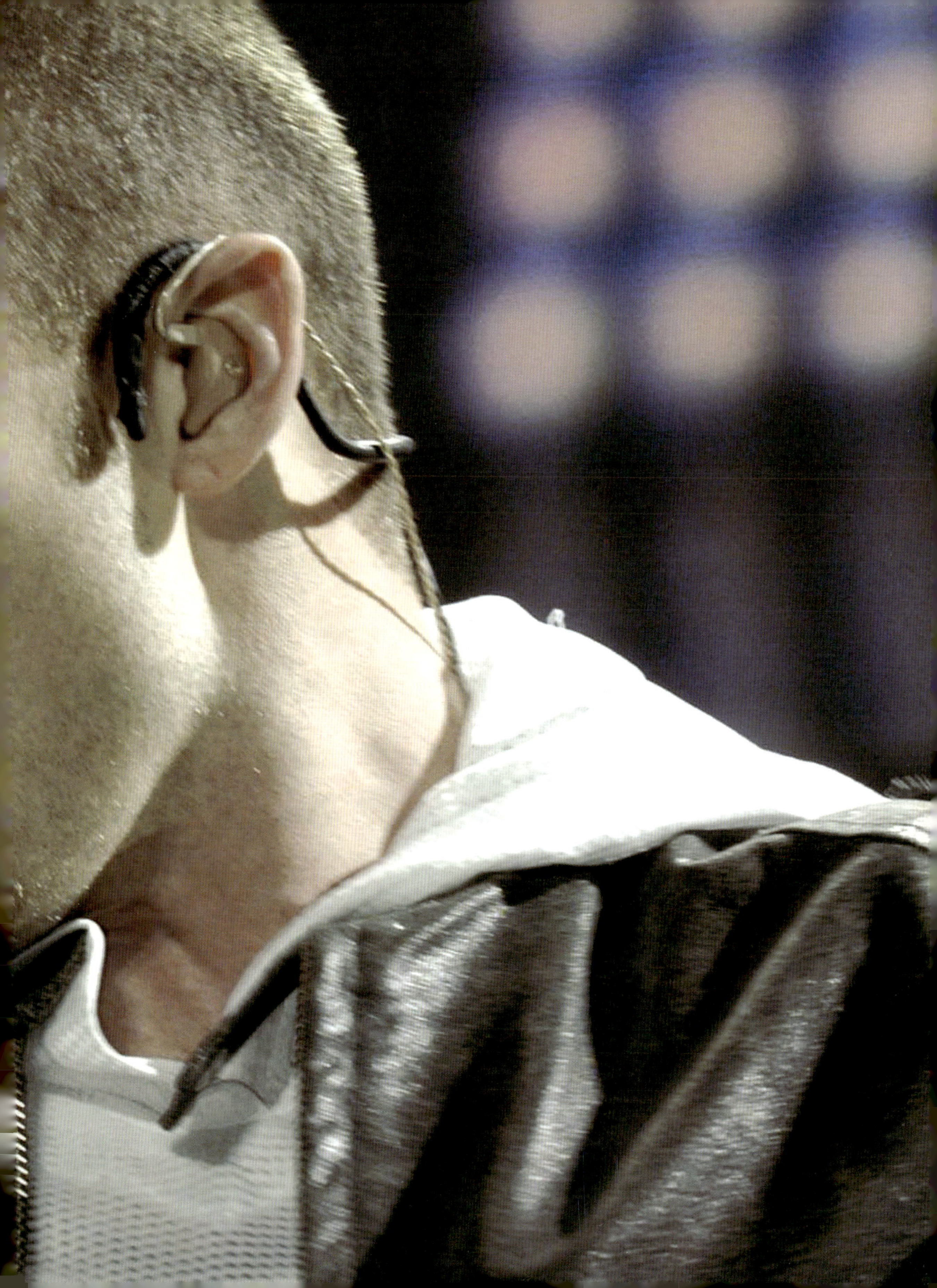

Britain has always had a special place in Justin's heart – and now he's gone solo he's spending even more time over here. The first few months of 2003 saw him stay longer in Britain than the previous few years put together. He just can't help causing a sensation wherever he goes and, in the week running up to an appearance on Ant and Dec's *Saturday Night Takeaway* in January 2003, he managed to cause quite a stir.

Arriving in the UK with an enormous entourage of minders, advisors and personal assistants, he checked into his hotel on Sunday evening, several days before his scheduled appearance. After a quiet night he spent Monday preparing for the hectic timetable ahead, running through the schedules with his record company. Next came a couple of days of radio and TV interviews as well as a chill-out massage session. He even told DJ Neil Fox that he was in negotiations to star in a remake of the film *Grease*.

Interviews with Capital FM and Radio 1 followed, and nightfall saw Justin hit the dance floor with a mystery blonde at trendy Browns nightclub. Tabloid reports claimed he hit it off with a 21-year-old student called Sarah-Jane and promptly installed her in his hotel suite. Naughty!

By Thursday, after a quick session with Trevor Nelson on hip satellite channel MTV Base, Justin was in need of some shopping therapy, so he hit Kensington's Urban Outfitters and sustained some serious damage to his wallet. Next

"Kylie's **very cool** and such an **intelligent, gorgeous** woman."

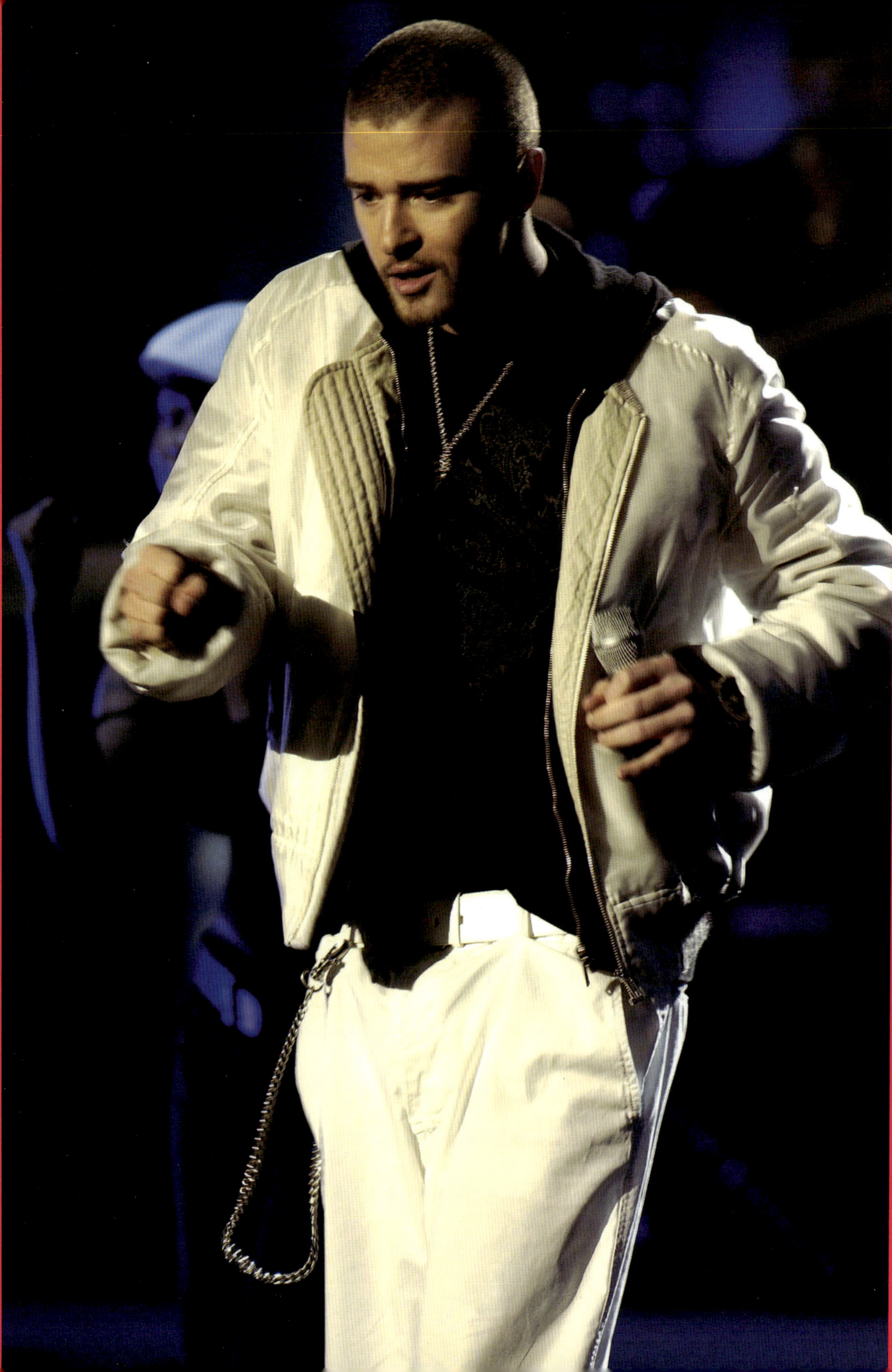

> "I've heard that people in Britain are **obsessed** with Kylie's bum – and I can **totally see why**. I'm pretty **obsessed** with it now, too."

stop was the BBC to film a surprise appearance on *Top Of The Pops*. But this time he wasn't singing his latest single, but playing bass guitar dressed as a dolphin!

Justin had reportedly met Wayne Coyne, frontman of indie band Flaming Lips, at Radio 1 and the pair got chatting. When Justin told him how much he liked their music, Wayne invited him to play bass with them on *TOTP* for the performance of their single 'Yoshimi Battles The Pink Robots Part 1'. Justin "porpoisefully" disguised himself in blue velour – the psychedelic rockers' trademark is to dress in a variety of animal suits – and remained under wraps until the latter part of the performance. But he clearly had a good laugh and proved he has the musical talent to go with the looks.

Friday morning brought another whirlwind of interviews and a recording of a slot for *The Saturday Show*. After another quiet night in at his hotel (or maybe he was entertaining...), Justin had to rise early for his live spot on *CD:UK*. He then dashed off to lunch at Planet Hollywood and momentarily lost his cool when hundreds of fans threatened to ruin a peaceful break. Justin-mania had hit Britain and Justin couldn't believe it!

Later that day he headed for an appearance on Ant and Dec's Saturday night show, but unfortunately for Justin (and possibly for Ant and Dec) his performance of 'Cry Me A River' was accompanied by the running of the final credits. Justin was apparently hopping mad at the time and had a face like thunder as he stormed into the green room "ranting and raving" his disapproval. He would never go on the Geordie double act's show again, reports said. After this tantrum worthy of a true diva, he flounced back to his hotel to change for a party being thrown in his honour at the Mayfair Club, where he was able to dance away his frustration.

February saw the staging of the 2003 Brit Awards – and Justin's now infamous duet with Australian popstrel Kylie Minogue. If Justin thought his British fans couldn't get enough of him, it was nothing compared to Kylie's enthusiasm for the new prince of pop! The duo appeared together for the awards ceremony held at Earl's Court and gave a sexually charged performance of Blondie's classic early-1980s chart-topper 'Rapture'.

The 5,000-strong audience witnessed the cheeky chap gyrate behind the pint-sized singer who was dressed in a sexy little black number. He then made a grab for Kylie's famous posterior. Speaking after his performance he said,

"She's got the hottest ass I've ever seen. I didn't just touch it – I copped a feel. On a scale of one to ten, it was a 58." He added: "I've heard that people in Britain are obsessed with Kylie's bum – and I can totally see why. I'm pretty obsessed with it now, too."

Justin may have been impressed, but Kylie's on-off ex-boyfriend James Gooding, who was watching in the audience, was said to be furious at Timberlake's amorous antics. Jealous James apparently stormed up to Kylie at an after-show party and accused her of flirting with Justin before being grabbed by minders and shown the exit.

Though Kylie wasn't up for an award, she'd agreed to make an appearance at the Brits and to do the much-publicised duet with Justin. If it was publicity she was after she couldn't have done better – the resulting furore in the British press ran for days afterwards and became the event's focus of attention, totally eclipsing the achievements of those like Missy Elliott who'd actually won an award.

Speculation ran rife on whether Justin had spent a night of passion with Kylie, her younger sister Dannii... or did he score a double and bed both Aussie songstresses?

So what did happen on the night? It seems that, after their steamy performance, Kylie and Justin left the ceremony with Kylie's little sis and had a meal at posh Montpeliano restaurant with friends. The girls then dashed off to the EMI after-show party held at London's Sanderson Hotel and, after a few hours chatting and dancing, Dannii left the party with Justin in his car. Said vehicle pulled up at the Mandarin Oriental Hotel, where the party was to continue in his suite.

And this is where the confusion sets in. Dannii supposedly went in with Justin, but it was later revealed the singer had stayed in the car and returned to her Battersea flat. Speculation then grew that Dannii was actually a decoy for her big sister... who, allegedly, had fancied Justin for ages! Stories circulated that Kylie had been smuggled through the back entrance and had left the hotel in the early hours, followed a few hours later by a bleary-eyed Justin looking decidedly the worse for wear.

However, neither sister will confess to what really happened. And why should they? Dannii revealed in a radio interview that she and Justin were just good mates. "The only thing that happened between me and Justin Timberlake is that I had dinner with him – and my sister! We had a wicked night running round with Kylie and then we all went to a party at the Sanderson, and then I caught a ride home in his car... but I didn't go into his hotel room at all." She added, "I fancy Justin when he's singing – I love it when he's doing his dancing thing. But when I was just chatting to him I was like 'It's just Justin'."

According to one tabloid paper Timberlake has come clean about the evening's events, suggesting a tryst with the elder Minogue. "Yes, we were in the hotel together. She came in late and we had some drinks. She was upset after her argument with James [Gooding] and I was there to look after her. Kylie's very cool and such an intelligent, gorgeous woman." So did anything happen or not? "I gave her sister, Dannii, a lift. But she didn't want to come in to the hotel for a drink and I went in alone. Then I got a call from Kylie and I said come to the hotel for a drink. That's all I want to say on the matter."

But the media frenzy didn't die down easily, especially when the news broke that, immediately after the Brits, Kylie had jetted to New York to be reunited with Justin at the Grammy Awards. As they stood together on the Madison Square Garden stage, which JT had previously graced as one fifth of *NSYNC, our lad saucily enquired, "Can I grab your ass again?" Miss Minogue was having none of it, playfully shrieking "no" as Justin made his advance.

Kylie later insisted that she only had eyes for her new fella – Olivier Martinez, a man the papers have dubbed the French Brad Pitt – admitting she's head over heels in love with him. "It was so great working with Justin," she revealed. "His talent is obvious and he's very down-to-earth. But my Olivier is even more lovely."

Justin has enjoyed being in London as a bachelor, but finds it hard to meet people because when he's here he's usually working. "The last time I was here I met up with Shaznay Lewis from All Saints, and Lance was over as well," he reveals, adding, "I appeared on *The Johnny Vaughan Show*. He's a pretty awesome guy – he makes me laugh." But clumsy Justin managed to miss the *Smash Hits* Poll Winners' Party after a fall. "Can you believe I broke my foot while 'breaking' some new moves?" he laughed.

Justin's a keen fan of British and Irish music. "I've met the guys from Westlife, they're cool guys, really nice. I think they have great voices. Also there's so much hype about Ms Dynamite, and I've heard a couple of her songs. I really like them. But obviously my favourite band in the whole world is Coldplay. I'm a huge Coldplay fan!" He's also confessed to loving the British accent.

Much to the disappointment of his American fans, Britain got the first chance to sample Justin performing as he kicked off his debut solo concert tour in the UK, beginning on 7 May 2003 in Sheffield and ending up at London's Wembley Arena ten days later. With only seven shows originally planned, tickets sold like hot cakes and it wasn't long before every venue was sold out. Though many performers had postponed tours of the UK because of the war with Iraq, Timberlake had been determined not to let his fans down. And there would soon be the chance to show appreciation...

"My **favourite** band in the whole world is Coldplay. I'm a **huge** Coldplay fan!"

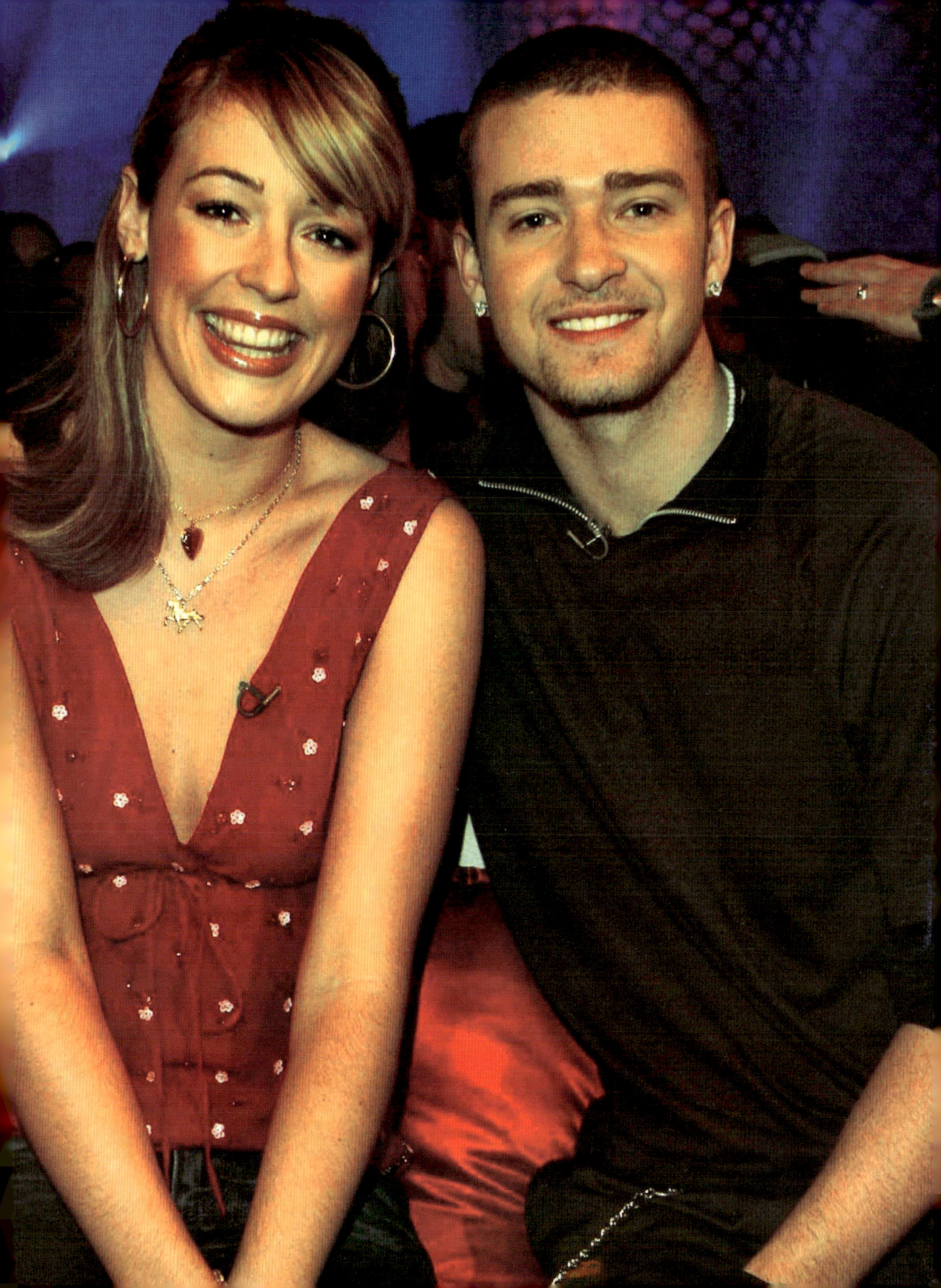

Justin's live debut set the tone for the tour as the 13,000 fans packed into Sheffield Arena rose as one to acclaim pop's hottest property. Hitting the stage to the strains of current single 'Rock Your Body', he soon revealed an outfit under his black leather jacket that was whiter than white – baggy trousers and a sleeveless, hooded top. Six more costume changes would follow! A radio microphone allowed Timberlake freedom of movement – and how he used it, climbing to a platform over the crowd's head to urge them to dance and go wild. Needless to say, they did just that!

The *NSYNC days got a nod with an affectionate medley of 'Gone' and 'Girlfriend': when he asked the (almost exclusively female) crowd "Will you be my girlfriend?", the response would have drowned out Concorde! Few of those present would dispute one critic's next day report that "Justin Timberlake is sex on legs..."

A surprise cover of Afrika Bambaataa's hip-hop classic 'Planet Rock' sat well alongside his own songs as Justin rampaged through his set, the ballad 'Still On My Brain' a welcome respite from the unrelenting dance tempo. 'Spectacular' was the word that came to mind as he jived on the piano, jumping down to perform a "reverse snake-charmer" trick, in which he appeared to make his microphone stand disappear into the stage. And there was more magic to come when, with loud bangs and flames, he disappeared himself in a puff of smoke. Fortunately, Justin survived for the encores!

The pattern continued throughout the country. Brooklyn Beckham, resplendent in a *Justified* T-shirt, attended the Manchester concert with his parents and cut a few moves that suggested he could be a rival in 15 years' time... Posh and David B took the star of the show – Justin, not Brooklyn! – to the swanky Living Room restaurant to round off the night (JT had a club sandwich and fries). And as Justin headed for London, where he and his entourage had taken over a whole floor of the swanky Mandarin Oriental Hotel, Prince Harry – no less – had been on the phone for tickets.

From royalty to the fan on the street, it is clear that Britain loves Justin Timberlake – and it seems the feeling is mutual. Why else would he have taken his first solo stage steps here? Maybe it's because *Justified* hit number one in the UK charts, beating his home country where it "only" reached number two. Or perhaps it's our audiences' uninhibited reaction to his music and moves?!

Whatever the reason, Justin warns us to watch out for him when he's over here, because the UK vibe makes him up for fun on a grand scale. Rest assured, if the success of his debut album and UK tour is anything to go by, he'll be hopping across the pond on a regular basis in the months and years to come. And who's going to complain at the chance of seeing even more of the sexy Mr Timberlake? Not us!

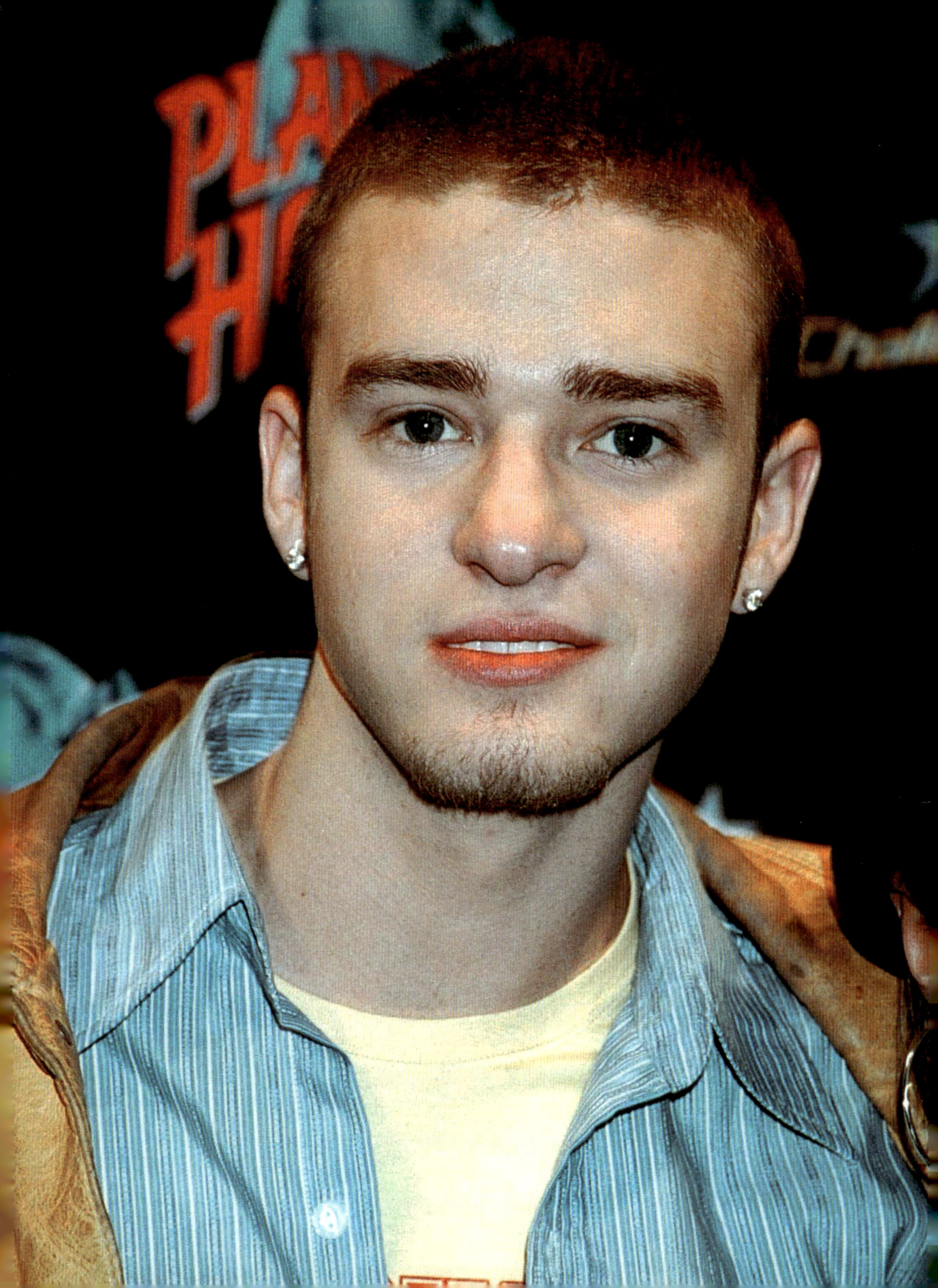

"I really **believe** that when you do something you should put **everything** into it; otherwise it's really **not worth it**."

Chapter Eight
CHILLIN' OUT

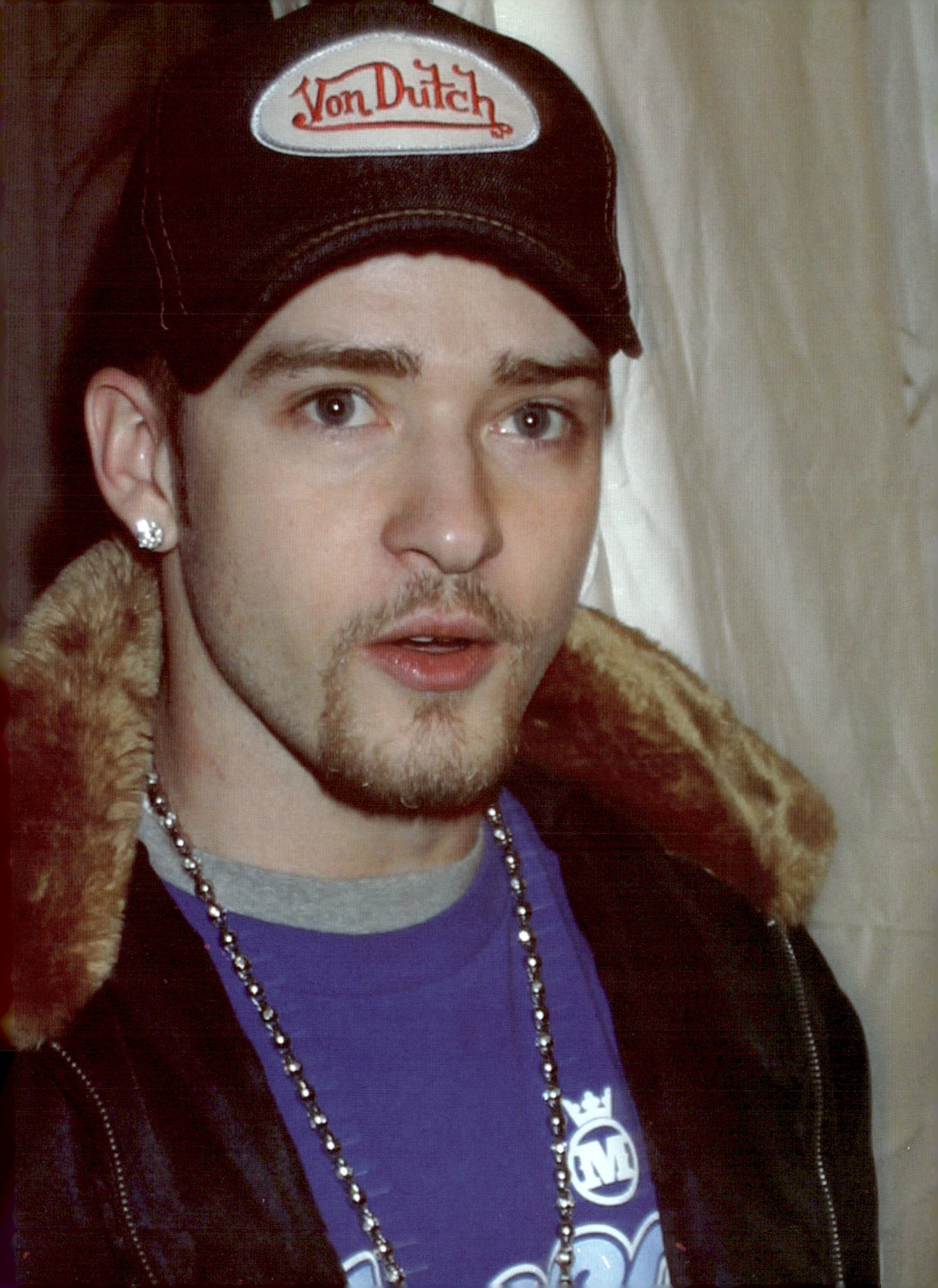
Von Dutch

It's not easy being a sex god, pop star and multi-talented musician all rolled into one. With everybody demanding a piece of him wherever he goes and his private life getting as many column inches as his professional life, Justin Timberlake really relishes the brief time he has to relax – away from the pressures that his superstar status brings. "When work overloads me I go and find some time for myself. Maybe I'll just light a candle, or I'll close my eyes or go and watch the sunset," he says wistfully.

He maintains that the person we see portrayed in the media and performing onstage is not the real Justin. "I think when I'm not working I am a different person. When I'm not working I don't like to think about work – I like to do simple things." He is at pains to point out that, though he is famous, he is just like any other person and finds it hard to understand why fans hold him up as some sort of idol. So will the real Justin Timberlake please step forward...

It is clear that Justin has always been very mature for his age. Though he is the junior partner of *NSYNC in age terms, his pop pals say he is the most reliable and trustworthy. "Justin is our youngest member, but he's also the most mature," said Chris over five years ago. "He's got a really good head on his shoulders. When it's time to work, he's always there to work. He's very responsible and he knows what's expected of him. That's really impressive, given that he's only 17."

This work ethic hasn't changed. Justin still prides himself on his dedication and commitment and feels that if something is worth doing it's worth doing well. "I'm just a very passionate person in everything I do," he admits. "I really believe that whenever you do something you should put everything into it; otherwise it's really not worth it." Justin reckons his best quality is his ability to make people laugh, though his most prized possession is his voice: "And I'm gonna look after it."

Looking at his flawless features and pleasant persona, it's hard to imagine Justin being anything other than perfect. Perfectionism is, in fact, his biggest fault, according to the man himself. "My perfectionism is something I have had to deal with. I've been to some crazy places in my head because I expect so much from myself. I've been in a hotel before and just cried for no reason, because I thought I could do so much at the same time."

He sees himself as an independent kind of guy and thinks it's easy for people to get the wrong impression of him. "I am a pretty quiet person and keep to myself a lot. It seems as if, over the years, if you see me when I'm not on stage I'm kind of shy. Sometimes I feel more comfortable on stage. If you see me and I don't say much, don't think I'm not taking in what you have to say – I'm just not a big talker."

Away from the glare of the cameras, Justin has an amazingly down-to-earth perspective on fame, fortune and everything that goes along with it. "It's easy to get sucked into it. You just have to remember who you are, and what is going to mean the most to you down the road. Are you going to look back and say, 'Yeah, I really had a good time'? Is it going to be worth it?"

He has a refreshingly philosophical approach to life for someone his age. "For me, this is like a calling," he says of pop stardom. "So many times I hear the word 'talent' when someone describes us [*NSYNC] or me, but I don't feel like it's a talent I've developed, so much as something God has given me. And when you have a calling like that, you're born to do it." When he sits down to write a song he admits that he often can't remember doing it and that it's almost like someone is sitting alongside him telling him what to write.

His faith in God has shaped his personality and has enabled him to remain compassionate and sympathetic to those less fortunate than himself. "I've had moments in my career, in the short career that I've had so far. The biggest moments to me are when you get to meet an underprivileged child or somebody with an illness or something and they come to you. We meet kids from the Make A Wish Foundation before every show and, to me, those are the greatest moments. When you get time to spend with someone one on one, and they tell you just how seeing you on television or hearing your song on the radio or buying your record affected their life."

He was brought up as a Baptist and, though he doesn't attend church, he still has a strong belief. "I think miracles happen every day. You know, I don't get a chance to go to church any more so some people might say I'm not as involved in my spirituality as them. That's so not true. I don't want any people to think I'm blasting the church. I'm just saying I can get the same experiences outside of church. I read my Bible but don't base my decisions on what the Bible says; I base my decisions on my experiences with God.

"I saw this T-shirt the other day that said, 'I'm not religious, I just love God.' I thought that was a cool little message. My spirituality is mine and I really don't want anyone to feel something that they don't want to feel. But my thing is God is all around us – in everything we say,

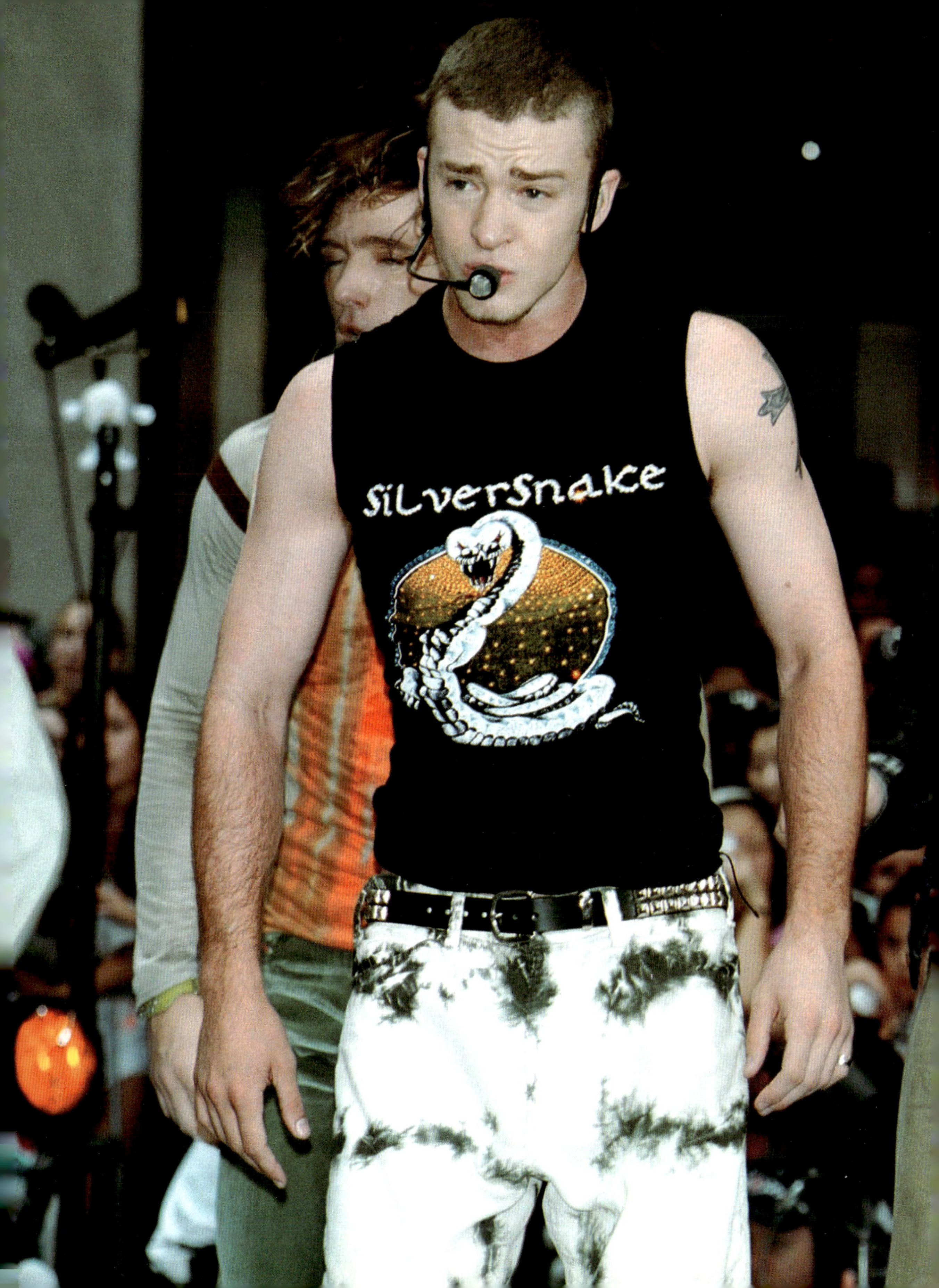
SiLverSnake

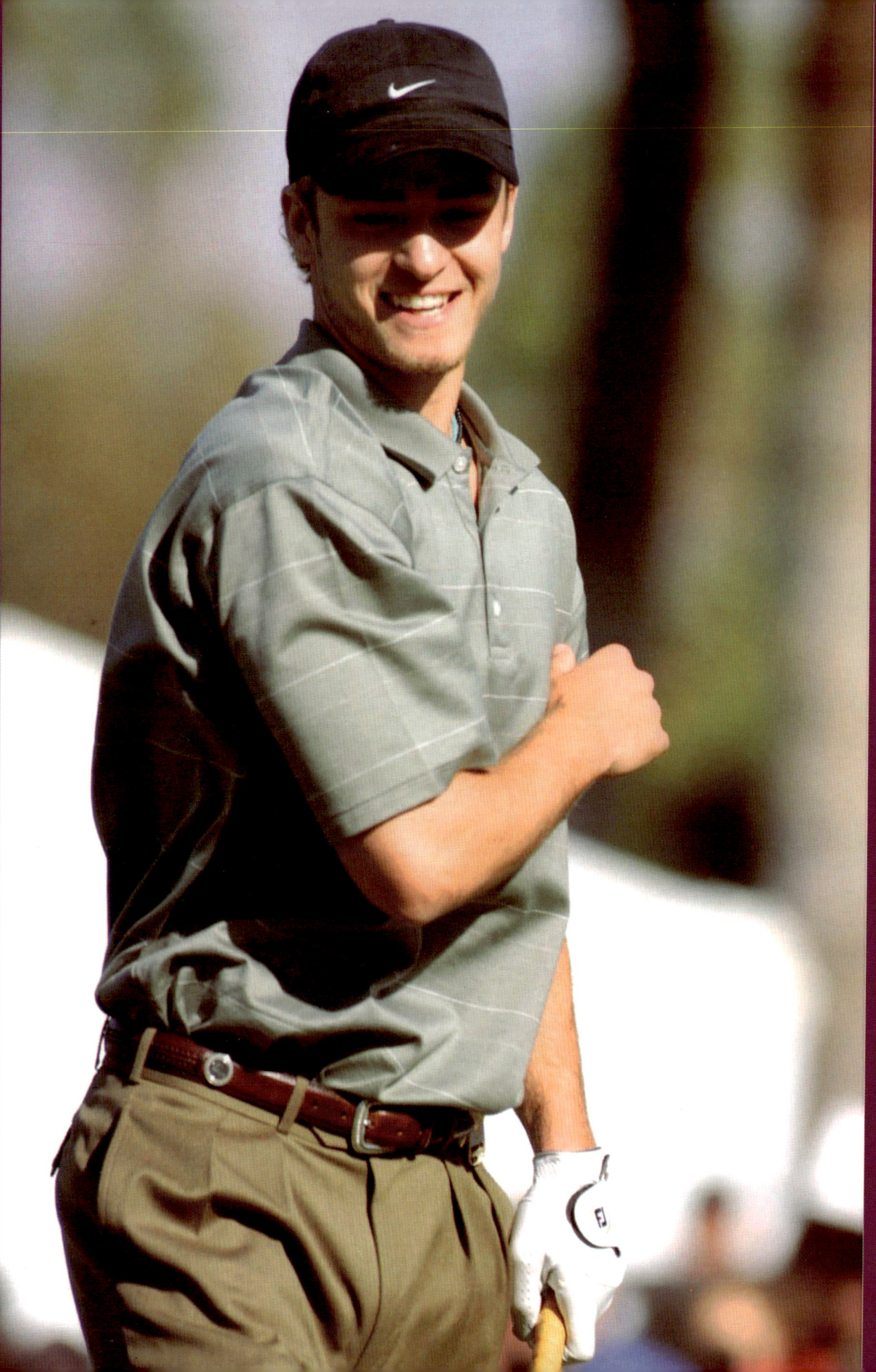

> "God is all **around** us – in everything we say, everything we do, everything we feel. I **really believe** that."

everything we do, everything we feel. I really believe that." Justin's favourite book is *Conversations With God*. "I've read one, two and three!" Nowadays he describes himself as spiritual rather than religious.

Despite his inner certainty, Justin confesses he can sometimes be superstitious. "I'm cautious about silly little things like walking under ladders. Even though in a way I don't believe in it, I kinda do believe at the same time. Say it's Friday the 13th and a black cat crosses your path... it's spooky, isn't it? When I'm driving, if ever I go through an amber light I try to make it across before it turns red. If I make it, I have to kiss my finger and touch the ceiling and then I get good luck."

He doesn't get heavy about horoscopes, though. "I don't look for my 'scope but if I'm flipping through a magazine and I see it I'll read it for fun. They're so vague that you can always relate it to something. I've never had a tarot-card reading before but, one time, we were shooting this thing for MTV and I got my palm read. She was pretty dead on and I was amazed." Astrology may not be Justin's bag but he obviously doesn't dismiss it completely... "I think I became so consumed with her [Britney] that I didn't see some of the things I should have. Britney's a fire sign, a Sagittarius, and they do things on a whim."

Born on 31 January, Justin is a typical Aquarian: sociable, fun-loving and great company. "He's always fun to hang around with and is up for whatever," says JC. "I'm a real party animal... when the others let me go to parties!" said Justin when the guys first started out.

Aquarians get on with everyone, have lots of friends and tend to be very popular with the opposite sex – all things that are true of the Southern charmer. Those born under the sign of the water bearer are often imaginative and inventive – and Justin has both these qualities by the bucketful if his debut album is anything to go by. It's a well-known fact that people born under air signs are charming and beautiful – so that must be where Justin gets it from! Aquarians are usually offbeat in their attitude to life, while their deep-seated need to achieve often means that they reach the very top of their chosen profession. No surprise then that Justin's currently the very hottest thing in pop. As his star sign suggests, Justin is very sure of himself and determined to succeed.

Family means everything to Justin, and he admits they've become even more important as he's got older. "I really value my family and friends. I like simple things," he explains. "I think that just growing up, your priorities change. Mine have changed drastically this year. My family and the people I love have become a big priority. You kind of take them for granted until you can't see them because of your career. I don't care what anyone says – you can have all these riches, and I'm happy with myself, but to have someone to share it with... you can't beat that."

Justin is famously close to his mum and reckons it'll be hard to meet a girl that matches up to her. "We have a special relationship. She's such a fun woman. When we go out together she often parties later than me." And, while she's not partying, she even does his ironing for him! "If she didn't I probably wouldn't worry about it too much. What's a few creased clothes?" says Justin. "Memphis is the most

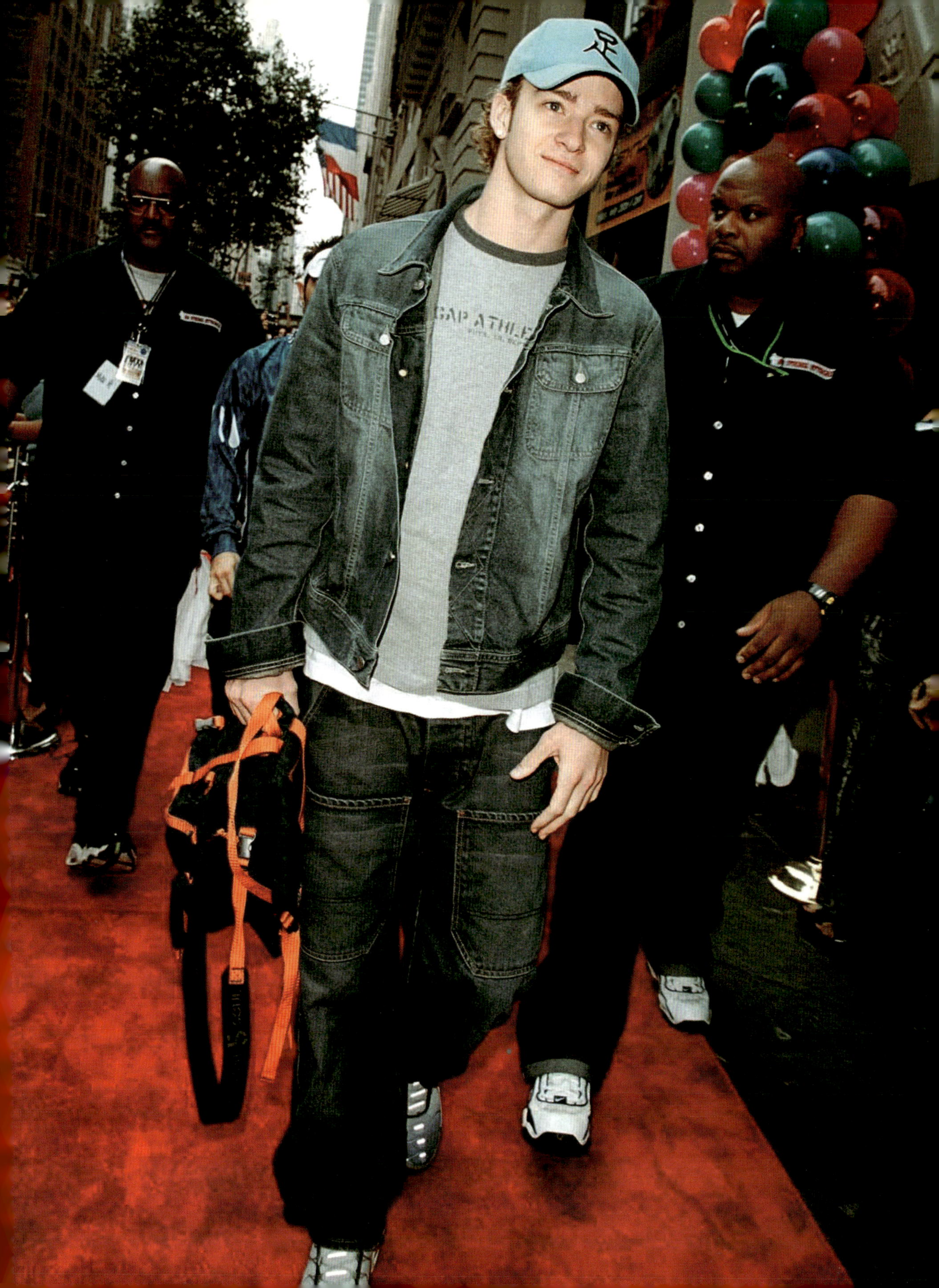
GAP ATHLE

homey place. It's not too big, and it's not too small. I'm like Dorothy in *The Wizard Of Oz*. There's no place like home."

Justin has many friends and they all love him to bits. His friends call him Curly (for obvious reasons) and Bounce and Shot (because of his passion for basketball). His best friend is Trace Ayala, whom he has known since childhood, and the pair often hang out in the yard shooting chunks of potato from homemade "spud guns". "It's a total country boy thing," Justin explains.

The lads from *NSYNC are more than just band members, too. "All five of us are friends. And that makes a big damn difference. There have been record companies that have put groups together and they don't work out, but we practically live together. If you're not friends, it's gonna show. We've had problems. But there's never been a problem we couldn't work out because we have that friendship. Even if we stopped selling records tomorrow, we'd still be friends."

The *NSYNCers all have their own handle on Justin's personality. "He's very creative," says Lance. "And he's goal oriented," reveals JC. Because they are so tight they are also comfortable pointing out his faults. "His most annoying trait is the way he talks to himself. Oh yeah, and the way he spaces out and totally goes off somewhere else," says Chris. Justin admits his worst personal habits are clearing his throat constantly and burping, though he insists he only burps in private!

Justin's a real foodie, too, and has a passion for cereal. His preferred brands are Apple Jacks and Oreo Os. "My all-time favourite though is the classic Captain Crunch. It's like a butter, honey-type cereal," Justin explains. He adores his granny Sadie Bomar's home cooking. "Whenever I come into town – I don't even have to tell her – she'll always make me a peach cobbler. And that's the closest to heaven I think I've ever been. She makes great pecan pie… she makes great everything. She's an incredible cook." Justin's favourite candy bar is Caramello and his top nosh is pasta. Food even features in his ideal night in with a date. "My perfect evening would be if a girl cooked me dinner cos I like to eat. And even if the food sucks it still shows how much effort she's put in it."

He may drive an expensive car, wear the most expensive clothes and stay in the most luxurious hotels, but Justin Timberlake insists he's a normal guy at heart. "What I know as normal is not what someone else knows as normal. But I don't really feel like I've missed out." He enjoys chilling out like most other lads his age do, playing games and hanging out with his mates.

But unlike most other guys his age, he has a purpose-built games room in his $5 million house. "I have a huge games room called the Funzone. I love Xbox and play a game called Halo that I'm addicted to. And golf games. We have game nights at my house and play board games like Cranium, Category and Pictionary." Justin reckons he's an ace at Scattergories. He also likes NBA 2K (a basketball computer game) and anything which features golf ace Tiger Woods.

Justin loves to duel pal and mentor R&B singer Brian McKnight on Xbox and PlayStation. "We're just like little boys," says Brian. He also loves going to the movies and enjoys films like *Scream*, *Titanic* and *The Usual Suspects*. He rates actors Jim Carrey, Samuel L. Jackson and Brad Pitt. "I really think Brad is one of the most underrated actors," says Justin. "I think he's incredible. But because he's a pretty face, a lot of people just don't look at him that way. They look at him as somebody who sells sex."

His favourite actresses are Sandra Bullock, Meg Ryan and Jennifer Aniston (*Friends* is one of his all-time favourite TV shows). He's even starred in a movie himself, playing a leading role in *Model Behavior* alongside Kathie Lee Gifford. Little wonder he's planning to install a customised theatre in his new mansion. "The screen will be massive and I'm gonna get a popcorn machine," he enthuses.

Justin's other great love is basketball, which he's followed since he was a young kid. Orlando Magic is his favourite team and Anfernee 'Penny' Hardaway (who also hails from Memphis) is his top player. "I watched Penny come up through the ranks at the University of Memphis, so I was a big fan of his before he came to play for the Magic," says Justin. He even has an autographed Shaquille O'Neal jersey he wouldn't part with for love or money and once said that, if he hadn't become a singer, he would have been a basketball player.

His all-time hero, though, is another of that breed – the great Michael Jordan. "Michael is my true idol," Justin

> "My **perfect evening** would be if a girl cooked me dinner cos I like to eat. And even if the food **sucks** it still shows how much **effort** she's put in it."

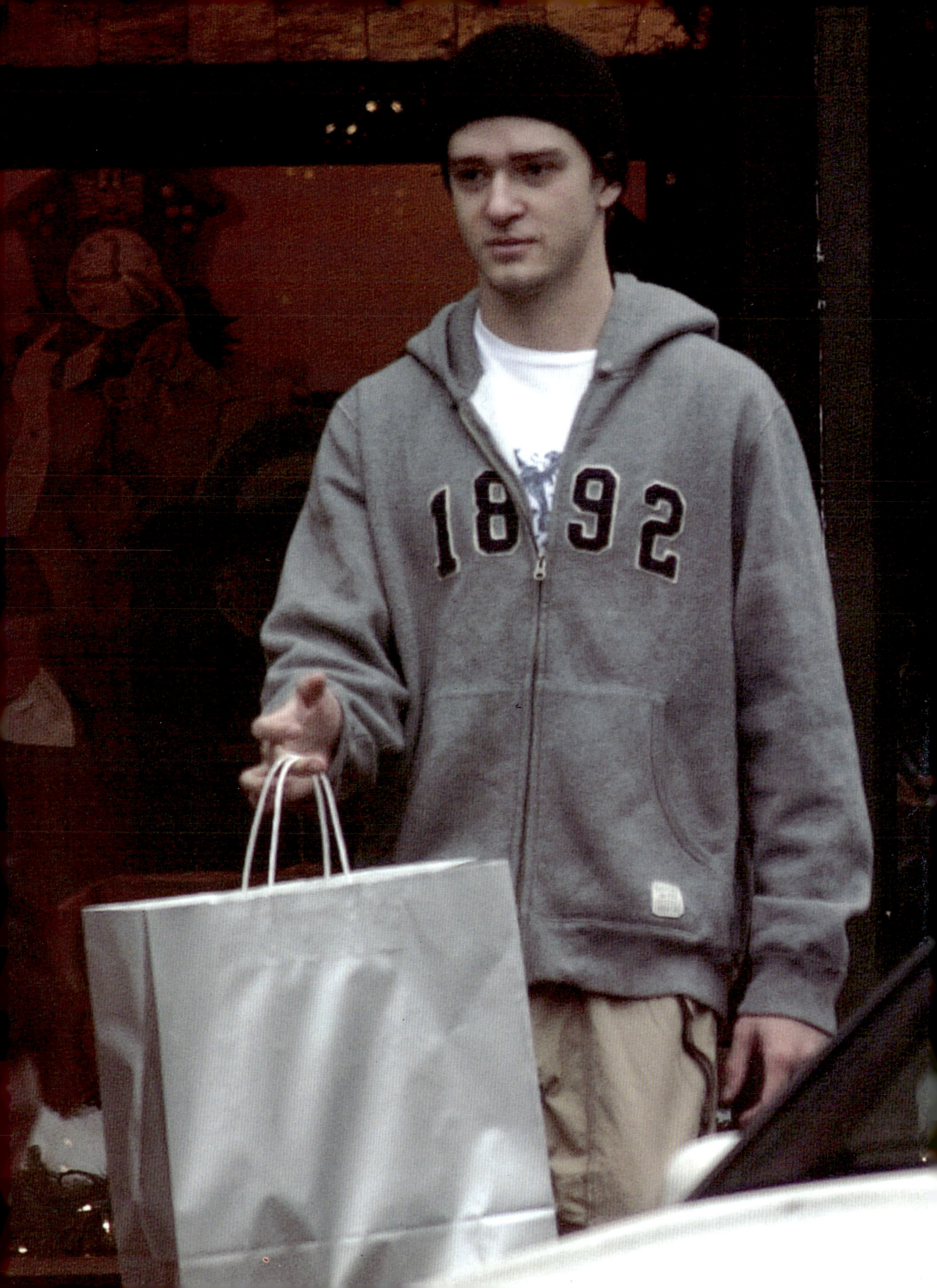
1892

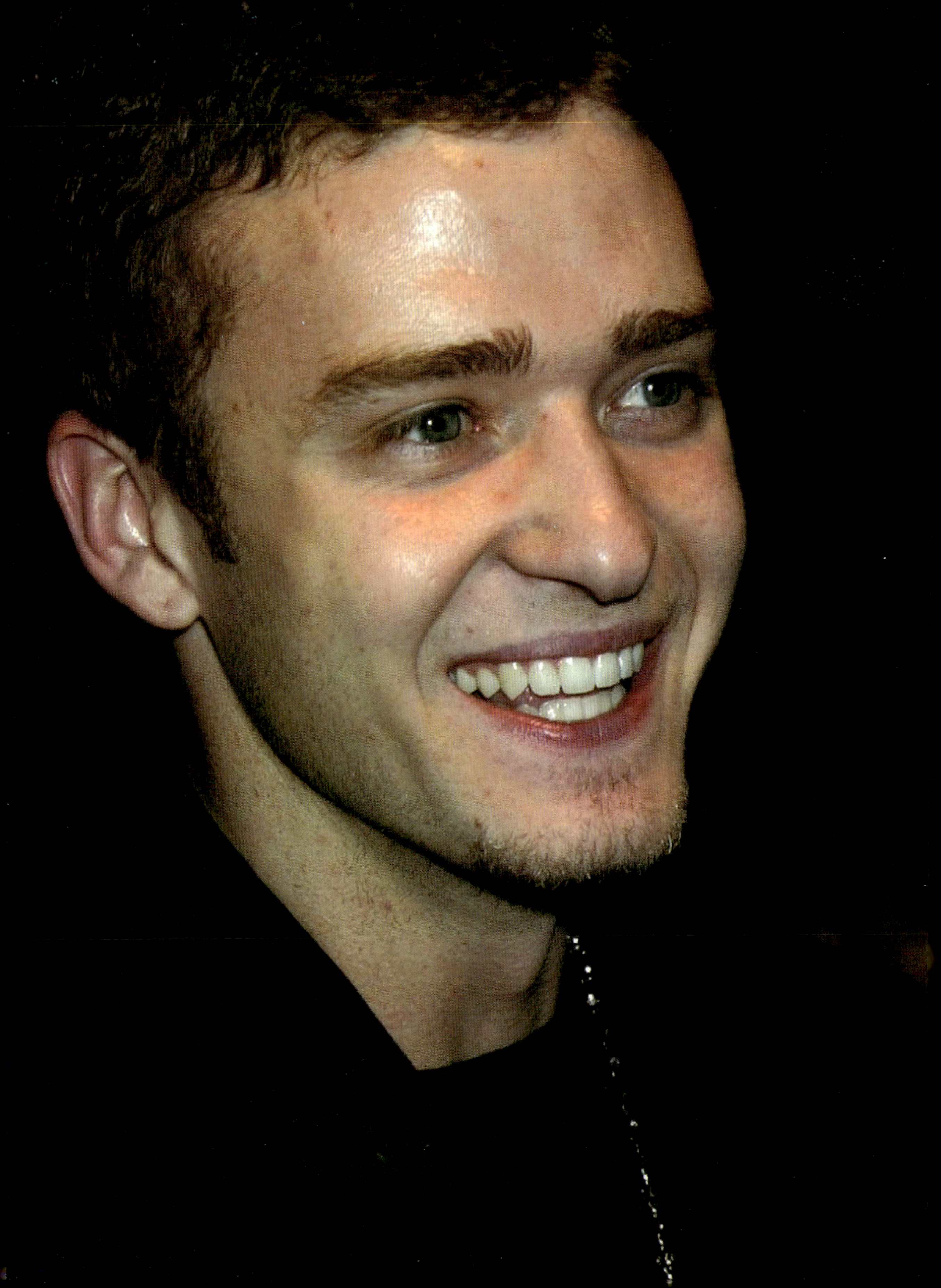

explains, "because of that look of determination in his eyes. It's that same look Tiger Woods has. It's that look where he won't accept losing. I have to admit I am a competitive person and a perfectionist. So I can relate to that."

When *NSYNC were invited to a private showing of Michael Jordan's movie, *Michael Jordan To The Max*, Justin was bowled over at the chance to talk to his idol face to face. "Meeting Michael made me completely starstruck. He's one of those people who seems like he doesn't really exist on this earth. It... put me out of my shoes for a second to be shaking hands with somebody that great."

Looking up to a sporting superstar like Jordan gave Justin the inspiration to succeed by setting his own goals. "Each time you reach a goal, you set another one. And you don't stop until you reach that goal. I think Michael Jordan's a perfect example of someone who uses himself as his own motivation and makes himself go out there and win."

Justin's a good all-rounder and is a pretty nifty basketball player himself. He's also good at golf. "I love basketball and whenever I've the chance I play like crazy. I'm a bit of a shopaholic, and collect North Carolina basketball gear." The most dangerous sport he's ever tried is a bungee jump, and he used to do in-line skating when he was younger.

When it comes to academic pursuits, Justin's no dumb blond either. He graduated high school a year early, even though he was working hard with *NSYNC at the time. His elementary school was so impressed with him that they retired his basketball jersey, Number 12, and his tutors awarded him his High School diploma in front of a crowd of 20,000 fans in his home town of Memphis. He reads avidly and his favourite author is John Grisham. The best book he's read is *Clue*, though he's into all sorts of books and will quote from self-help books like *Men Are From Mars, Women Are From Venus* at the drop of a hat. He even began writing a novel himself once.

Pop heart-throb or not, Justin has clear ideas on what he would and wouldn't do for money. Posing nude is a definite no-no! His biggest hates are fake people who are dishonest, his curly hair (which is why he shaved it off), girls who smoke (oops, Britney's blown it again!) and racism. His biggest fear is coming face to face with a snake or shark. "I'm really frightened of sharks. I mean, the stories I hear about sharks attacking people and the fact that it could actually happen to me is scary! And spiders and snakes, they gross me out. I think it's the s's. Snakes, sharks and spiders." But he's a softie at heart and loves most animals. He even has a pet dog (a Cairn Terrier) named Ozzie, and a cat named Alley.

Justin is terrified of flying and recently had a frightening experience when on a flight to Tokyo, Japan. Thirty minutes after take-off one of the Jumbo's engines was hit by a bird. The pilot decided to return to Los Angeles after trying to calm the panicking passengers. Justin and his fellow travellers were badly shaken by the incident.

One of our man's favourite hobbies when he's not working is to catch up on his sleep. Apparently he has a habit of talking in his sleep – his mother says you could even have a full conversation with him. She says she can ask him questions when he's in dreamland, because he will answer anything and that it's the best way to find out things about him!

Justin admits he sometimes suffers from not being able to sleep but he doesn't let it get to him. "Insomnia comes, but I just embrace it. I roll with it because you never know – that could be when the next hit song comes up. Everything in my life, I never shielded myself from it. I've just embraced it. It's like meditation: the more you know about your mind, the easier it is to deal with." If he can't fall asleep, he sometimes sings softly to himself or listens to music. He's also not a heavy sleeper. According to him, if someone were to stand over him or there's the slightest noise, he wakes up immediately.

Though Justin is generally happy with his lot in life – "I'm just comfortable being who I am," he says – he does suffer from a lack of self-esteem and reveals that his greatest fear of all is dying unloved. Luckily, that's one thing he doesn't have to worry about, because millions of fans everywhere have his face pinned on their walls. The poster boy has a lot of life left in him yet!

> "Meeting Michael [Jordan] made me completely **starstruck**. He's one of those people who seems like he doesn't **really exist** on this earth. It put me out of my shoes to be shaking hands with somebody that **great**."

Chapter Nine
THE
FUTURE

"I mean, maybe it's **pretentious** to say so, but I really do think I could **achieve** anything."

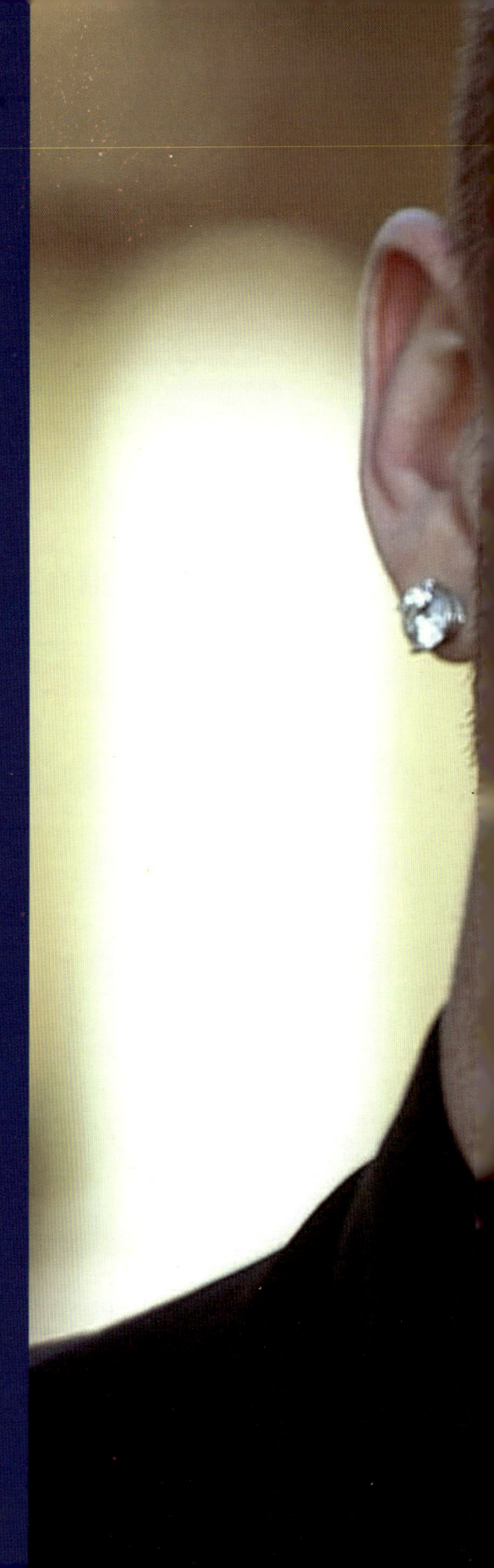

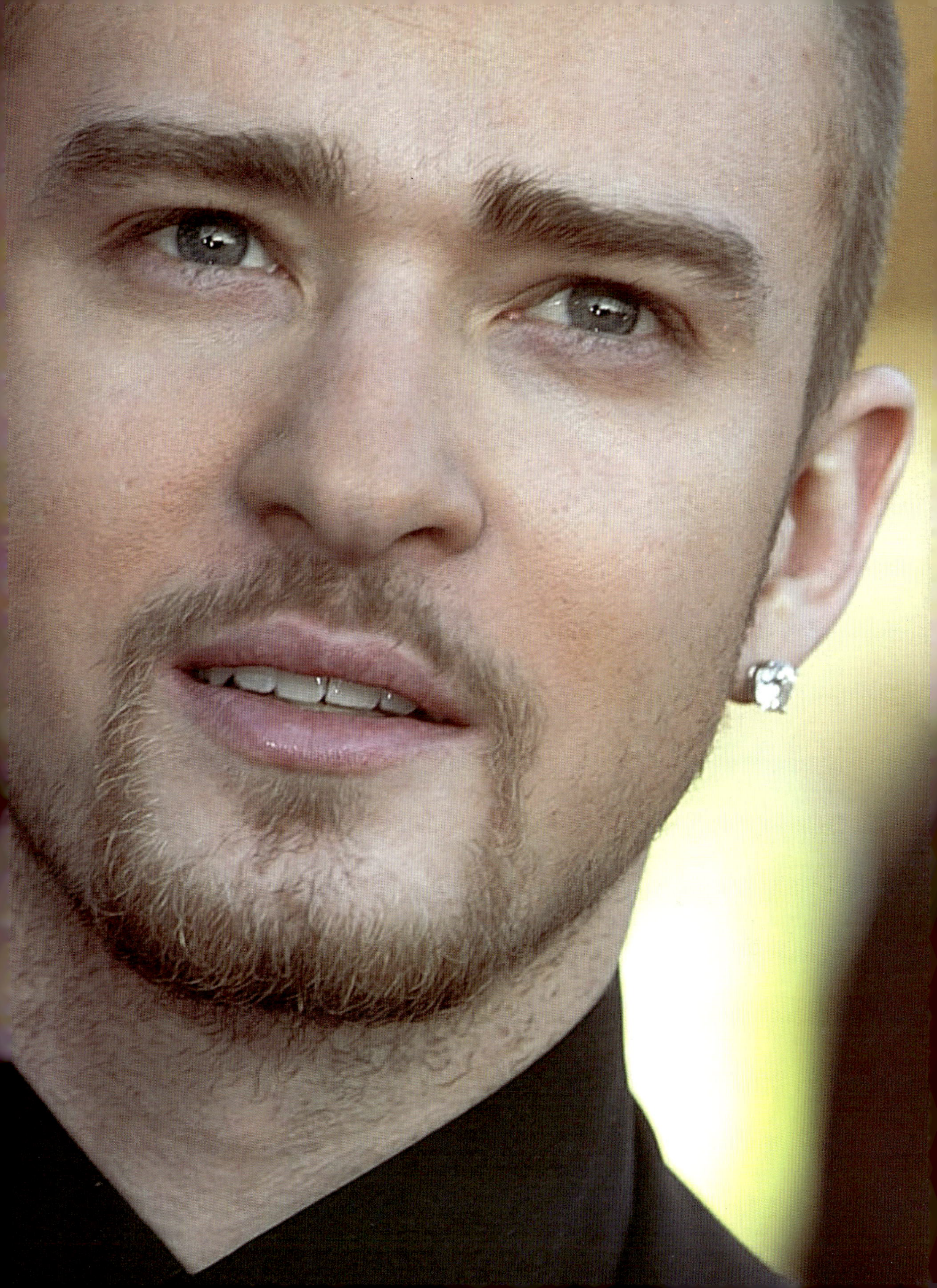

Justin's success as a solo player, both musically and romantically, poses many questions the world wants answered. Will he ever perform as part of *NSYNC again? Is his romance with Britney Spears well and truly over? Is he about to become the next Brad Pitt? Is he destined to be as successful as his inspiration, Michael Jackson?

His career to date has proved unquestionably that Justin Timberlake is definitely more than the sum of his boyband parts. His star is burning brightly in the pop universe and he looks set to eclipse nearly every other singer around him in the years to come. Everyone wants a piece of him – his music, his opinions and his private life! Justin-mania has arrived, and the media frenzy that goes with it is already in full swing. Justin has graced the covers of numerous magazines – women's, men's and music – and you'd better believe that there are many more in the pipeline.

Tabloid interest is at fever pitch, with barely a day going by where Justin doesn't warrant a few column inches. But for Justin Timberlake this is all part and parcel of becoming an international star. He says his biggest achievement to date is being taken seriously as a musician, and it is this that makes it easier to stomach the gossip and the reporters who still want to dig for dirt. "Regardless of what you do, rumours are gonna be around," he says philosophically.

The future looks bright for the Southern singer. His album reached number two in the US and number one in the UK. 'Cry Me A River', the second solo single, peaked at three in the States and two in the UK; while the advent of third single 'Rock Your Body' helped *Justified* hit the top spot in Britain one more time in May 2003. With a second spell at the summit in March to his credit, he was the first artist to have enjoyed three separate album chart reigns since Shania Twain in 1999, with UK sales of 826,000 to his credit.

He has made appearances with various internationally successful singers like Celine Dion and Elton John, and also performed at the Nickelodeon Kids' Choice gig. Musically he's bigger than he's ever been, while artistically he's won the respect of music critics the world over. He scooped the award for Best Chart Act at the DanceStar USA event held as part of the Miami Winter Music Conference. With a hit album and two major tours, 2003 proved to be 'Justin's Year' – just as certainly as 1998 was *NSYNC's.

But what of the future with the group that made his fame and fortune? Will *NSYNC stay together now that Justin's solo career has soared? He is adamant that this is not the end. "By no means are we going to break up," he insists.

"I think that's ridiculous. I initially felt an uneasiness about being on my own, because I didn't want the guys to think I wanted to leave the group. Those guys are my friends and we'll always be together."

He says that the difference between other "manufactured" outfits and *NSYNC is that they were all friends before they formed the group. "I don't think it will be weird to go back to the band. We've made a lot of music together for so long. We are friends. I don't see us as *NSYNC but as Lance, JC, Chris and Joey. Those are my friends, and when I'm 70 years old I'll still be in touch with them."

*NSYNC fans may have to wait a while before the band make another album, though, as at the moment all are doing their own thing. Lance, the "furthest out" of the five, has successfully completed a space-training course in Russia and, if all goes well, could be on course to become the first boyband member to leave the earth's atmosphere. Justin is proud of his friend. "I think it's amazing – such an incredible experience for him and a great challenge," he enthuses. "As much as people think it's hilarious, what if he actually goes? [If I was him] I'd be flying back from the moon giving everyone the finger." Lance is also running his own production company.

Joey Fatone has appeared in the hit movie *My Big Fat Greek Wedding* and on Broadway in the stage show *Rent*. "Seeing Joey revive Broadway is incredible." JC's released a single and is in the studio finishing his own debut album at the time of writing, while Chris has just signed up to manage Dallas band Ohno. "I think it's good, what everybody is doing," Justin says.

If he is riding his solo adventure because he thinks the boyband bubble has burst, he's not letting on. "I can't tell you what the trend is going to be tomorrow, and I don't feel that *NSYNC is just a trend. All we can do is the music that we feel. I think it spoils the creativity when you have to take external things into consideration. So my attitude is screw it, just write the song and record it, you know? If it feels good, do it."

Rumours of Justin's imminent departure from the band have been rife since his meteoric rise to solo stardom, but his friends have no doubts that Justin will remain a part of the quintet. "*NSYNC are a great band and I don't think Justin would leave them in the dark like that," said pal Billy Crawford, adding, "He's a good guy and he's a friend to them and it's not even about selling albums for him. I just think that he's gonna be there."

"By no means are we going to break up. I think **that's ridiculous**. Those guys are my friends and we'll **always** be together."

Justin agrees. "We will remain and be friends regardless of whether we make another album or not. But yeah, we're definitely going to make another record," says Justin. "Hopefully we'll be back in the studio early next year [2004] to record a new album."

The news is that the boys will indeed be back in the recording studio around that time and have begun coming up with material for a new album. "We've already started writing," says Lance. "JC and Justin have been writing a lot and we are going to have stuff that didn't make their albums, stuff that's more *NSYNC in style, so I don't know what direction this will go. It will definitely be interesting."

Whether *NSYNC will produce another album as a quintet remains to be seen, but fans can console themselves with the fact that they'll be seeing plenty more from Mr Timberlake. After his sellout UK tour he embarked on the highly publicised Justified And Stripped Tour with erstwhile Mouseketeer (and Britney's arch-rival) Christina Aguilera, which kicked off in June in Phoenix, Arizona. The summer-long 37-date trek promised to be a real spectacle. "It was an idea both our managers concocted," explained Justin. "When they came to me with the idea I said I was really interested. I thought it would be fun to tour with someone that talented."

Justin thinks Christina is fantastic, but had no fear of being upstaged by the pop minx. "I'm gonna make the arena feel like a club," he enthused. "I want people to feel like they're part of the show and it's a party. Anyone who sits down will get kicked out. If you sit down, once I find you, you will get booted," he threatened.

Christina was equally enthusiastic. "I'm so excited to be touring again and to be on stage performing for my fans. That's what makes it all worthwhile for me," she remarked. "I'm really looking forward to working with Justin. We are going to put on an unbelievable show. Get ready. This is something you don't want to miss."

Aguilera isn't the only pop star Justin would like to collaborate with. He has a list as long as his hit records including Lenny Kravitz, Madonna, Jay-Z and Coldplay's Chris Martin. "I'd love to do a duet with Chris. To me, Radiohead and Coldplay are the modern-day Beatles. I don't know if that would ever work but it would just be fun for me because I love his voice and I think he's a truly talented singer... and I know I could pull it off. It may not happen, but it doesn't hurt to put it out there. I could sit here and name a million artists that I would love to collaborate with and they would all be unique collaborations for their own reason."

Not all his collaborations have worked so far. When rockers NERD introduced him as a surprise guest on a radio show, poor Justin was booed – though it didn't appear to bother him. "I expected worse," he laughed. "That's not really my crowd. Anyone that boos me I feel the need to win them over. So maybe I'll do a rock album in a couple of years, curse all over the place so people will think I'm cool."

Hollywood beckons, too – maybe that's why he's already bought a house there. He has already appeared (as a model) in the movie *Model Behavior* and would like to make more films. "If I did something on the screen, I think it would have a light-hearted approach. It would have a comedic approach. That's the kind of training I had when I was on the *New Mickey Mouse Club*. It was skits, sketch comedy." In early 2003 he made a cameo appearance on rapper Nelly's single 'Work It', the video to which was shot at Hugh Hefner's Playboy Mansion. It featured Justin and Nelly playing tennis and pool, surrounded by scantily clad women. "It was fun. I was only there the first day because scheduling is always crazy. But I heard that on the second and third days there were topless women and all kinds of crazy stuff going on. I'm sad that I missed that, but, you know, such is life," sighs Justin.

He's been sent the script to *Grease III* and it's thought that he will play the part of Danny made famous by John Travolta. But who will play Sandy is anyone's guess... though we have to say that Britney would be his perfect on-screen partner. He has even had a couple of ideas of his own for screenplays. "I'm open to anything. I'm just having fun doing what I'm doing... I'm sure the critics will tell me how much I suck at it and it won't matter because I'll be having fun."

At the end of the day, though, making music is what drives Justin Timberlake. We can be confident that he will continue to indulge his passion for pushing artistic boundaries for many years to come. This is a man who is determined to make his mark as a lasting force in a business that is forever fickle and often unforgiving. Many of those who know him well have long acknowledged that Justin is bigger than just a teen phenomenon and has what it takes to go all the way. "This kid," says R&B impresario Silas White, "is one of those special artists who comes along every so often and changes everything. He will be one of the greats."

Producer Pharrell Williams gets to the essence of Justin when he says, "My boy just is what he is. He's got music." Justin says his success hasn't fallen in his lap by accident. "I think the secret to my success is that I don't do anything halfway. I think what matters is dedication and being at the heart of the matter, and having the diligence to carry through. I think that's why I'm where I am today. Whatever your dream is, you have to practise your craft and make it the best it can possibly be."

In a recent interview, Justin said he had finally come through the dark tunnel that engulfed him after the break-up with Britney. "I'm as happy as a lark and I feel like I have some peace." He worries whether he'll need that kind of drama again to make any future records. "It's going to be interesting to see what the next album is like because I'm in a different place now," he says. Justin has achieved his lifelong dream – so what goal has he set himself next? He certainly hasn't lost his focused ambition, despite his phenomenal success. He says, "I mean, maybe it's pretentious to say so, but I really do think I could achieve anything." The sky's the limit, Justin!

As far as the future is concerned, Justin really only has one wish. "I just want to be happy doing what I'm doing," he says. "If it all stops tomorrow, look at all the stuff that I can say that I've done. Maybe one day it'll slow down, but I'm on the ride right now." And boy, what a ride it's turning out to be...

"Maybe one day it'll **slow** down, but I'm on the **ride** right now."